Jotos del Barrio

Jotos del Barrio

a play by **Jesús Alonzo**
foreword by Anel I. Flores

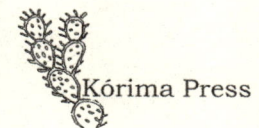

Kórima Press

Cover Art: Toni Sauceda
Title: "Jotos del Barrio"
Medium: 14x17 on bristol, mixed media
Date: May 27, 2014
Photographed by -JPL PRO- Julián Pablo Ledezma

Author Photo: -JPL PRO- Julián Pablo Ledezma

Published by Kórima Press
San Francisco, CA
www.korimapress.com

ISBN: 978-0692218921

This book is dedicated to Manuel Solis, María Alejandra Ibarra, and Erica Salazar, who fearlessly took on the work in its original form and brought it to life in a way that I never imagined; their simple brilliance will forever run through the veins of Jotos del Barrio.

Contents

Foreword

Queena of the Butterflies,
a narrative foreword

by Anel I. Flores

1993

My mother and father have decided I am not live anymore. At least that is what it feels like now that they know I am a lesbian. I am sixteen years old and although I know I am a queer emerging writer, the stories I will write as I grow into my true lesbiana, Mexicana, Chicana corazón are packed away in the same old suitcase Jesús Alonzo's character speaks about in his uncompromisingly fearless play, *Jotos del Barrio*. My suitcase is covered in fine gray south borderland barrio dust, hidden under my bed.

> The secret compartment of this suitcase tenderly stows the experiences of my first true love.... The memories of Olmos Park on Sundays; the cruisy trails of McAllister Park and Acequia Park over by the old missions; the Esperanza Peace and Justice Center and the Jump-Start Theatre, along with other openly queer friendly spaces also fill the liners of this suitcase. In the outside pockets, I stuffed all the hurtful names and judgments passed upon me along with all the fears I ever experienced. (Act I, Scene 1)

I only have a few more months in my parent's house. This summer I will realize they are done with me after 8 months of silent meals, avoided eye contact and complete apathy towards everything about me. I will pull my suitcase out from under the bed I shared with my sister for 17 years, slide my index finger across the top of the dust and put it up to my tongue to taste. The sweet, citrus memory of childhood-play and wind coming in from Mexico awaken in me the realization that the contents of my suitcase are the contents of my home, my barrio.

I start volunteering at Jump-Start Performance Co. and the Esperanza Peace and Justice Center (the Esperanza) so I can meet some queer friends. It is scary for me going to and from my dorm room to my car because it has already been vandalized with the words dyke, slut and puta. Dog shit was smeared on all of my door handles in the morning when I woke up before going into work at the Taco House. The president of my University has denied the LGBT club I want to start, before I even get a chance to submit the constitution to Student Government. My girlfriend's mother has threatened my life and called me a bitch and whore to my face. The only time I heard the word lesbian and Mexican in the same sentence was during the controversy over Selena Quintanilla's murder by the accused lesbian Yolanda Saldivar. The bars on Main St. become my safe place along with my drag and transgender sisters. I meet the late Miss International Queen, Erika Andrews, who tells me she feels like a "monster," at the MAC counter at Dillard's and witnesses the puffed hair, over primped perfume attendants point fingers at her and whisper. My insides are twisting in knots and each time we are lashed at, the feelings harden and petrify into stones. This is all happening because I decide to open up the contents of my suitcase. I am not the only one opening my suitcase. Jesús Alonzo's first draft of *Jotos del Barrio* is shared in a staged reading at the Esperanza. Even though the word joto still rings in my mind as a cruel word, I grab my suitcase and go to the theater. I was nervous as hell. I felt like no one wanted to sit near me because I was "uno de aquellos." Then, the lights go down in the theater and my shoulders and gut, which I had been holding in, relax. I finally feel safe in the dark. When, by surprise el joto slithers like a serpent off the stage y entra en lo más profundo de mis entrañas.

> The new man who comes out / is the same, same one / who once hid inside a frail boy. / But now he is out / and about / and without shame. / Sin vergüenza.
>
> ―
>
> Gay Xicano Man / dances. / Gay Xicano Man / sings. / Gay Xicano Man / writes the poems that turn into the / verses
> (Act I, Scene 2)

He introduces us to another voice, among a collage of voices, interrelated characters, who will rise from each scene proclaiming their feelings toward the *jotos del barrio* in their lives, some maligning and some exalting. "Sin vergüenza," the "Gay Xicano Man" exclaims his testimony of resistance against the shame connected to his once "frail" body signifying one movement upward on the lifelong flight he is about to mount. I meet the Joto's Amá y "papacito lindo" on the stage of the Esperanza, who speak Spanglish to their mi'jo, Tony, and hear conversations about being queer in the cruel and romantic language of the barrio, the border, our Tejas y México. His mother asks, what I will replay in my prayers for the next 20 years, "Hoy preguntas / Si a un hijo homosexual / Puedo yo amar // Esta es mi respuesta // Seas lo que seas / Hagas lo que hagas / Eternamente te amaré." (Act I, Scene 4) In an all-Spanish monologue Alonzo delivers a tender poem from the Mexicana mother's perspective, to her son, paralleling the cultural significance the Madre has for each child in our barrio. We are a people who fall to our knees in front of the mother of Mexico, La Virgen de Guadalupe, Tonantzin. We are a people who grow rosas in our garden to deliver on our knees to the Guadalupe church on El Paso Street on Mother's Day. We are a people who know, seek and believe our Madre, Mami, Amá is the queen of our corazón and whom we long for approval from. And, for many of us, we are young jot@s who have been taught that English is the "safe" language to speak, thus making it even harder for us to communicate our truths to our parents who only speak Spanish, "I can say / 'Mamá, soy marica, maricón, / joto, chifladito, curiosito, / invertido, un sodomita, / un ninfo, un perverso, un putito, / una loca, una vieja,'" (Act I, Scene 4) but the words in spanish to describe the celebrated and reclaimed word, joto, all have derogitory weight behind them and messages that we are sexual predators, perverts, abusers and crazy. And, although Alonzo takes me on a ride home, all I can focus on is the fact that my mother has told me I am going to hell and I am a disgrace to the familia y la iglesia.

2000-2003

My mother still won't admit I am gay. She says all my lovers are friends. The male coaches at the school where I teach think it is funny to say, "I love to look at her ass in those red pants," when our youngish principal walks by. I take a workshop with author, Sharon Bridgforth, and she tells me to write down the name of the person I am afraid to hurt with my writing. On a piece of paper, I write the word, "mami," right before she tells me to throw it in the trashcan and do this each time I am about to write my story. The theatrical performance of *Jotos del Barrio* is unleashed on the Jump-Start stage. Alonzo's craft brings forth fierceness. The audience sits at the dresser with Janie la Transie –played by none other than Erika Andrews– when she says, "I am my own creation; my very own work of art. Style is my sustenance, glamour my biological make-up. But I wasn't always like this. My real name is Juan Navarro, but that's what they called me when I was still my mommy's hombrecito. Whatever that means." (Act II, Scene 2) We sympathize for the Reminiscent Joto who is too weak to stand up to the Foolish Man who makes fun of a young joto on the bus. (Act 2, Scene 5) And we witness the innovative and rhythmic poetry that dances off the tongue like a queena entaconada y cantando Thalía's, "¿A quién le importa lo que yo haga? / ¿A quién le importa lo que yo diga? / Yo soy así, así seguiré, / nunca cambiaré." Each performance filled the theater beyond capacity and audience members lined the walls standing through the entire performance braiding tears and laughter into a strong mechate of memorials.

2004-2012

Alonzo and I teach *La Pluma El Corazón*, a creative writing workshop for jot@s of color. A white woman storms into our workshop on the second day and verbally attacks us by saying our class is racist and leaving people out. I begin writing my book, *Empanada: a Lesbiana Story en Probaditas*, which I gathered the tenacity to complete because of fierce jot@ work like Jesús' and many other amazing authors paving the way. We become closer and closer friends, writing together, sharing together, dreaming together, encouraging one another and reading together. *Jotos de Barrio* is brought up in conversation in jot@ circles each year, over and over in different cities, among different communities, even when Jesús is not around. In 2012, two teenage lesbians Mollie Olgin, 19, and her partner, Mary Christine Chapa, 18, were found with gunshot wounds to the head in a South Texas park, with one of them dying from her injuries. The murderer is never found. *"When will you publish Jotos, Jesús? When? Our jotos need it,"* many would cry!

2013-2014

On March 11th, 2013, actor, queena, sister, friend and drag mother, Erika Andrews dies. San Antonio, Texas and the international drag community are stunned and heartbroken. My mom still doesn't say the word gay even though 17 states have legalized gay marriage. The Obama Administration has deported more immigrants annually than the George W. Bush Administration and San Antonio passes the LGBT Non Discrimination ordinance after Austin, Dallas, Fort Worth, Houston, El Paso and more than 170 other cities nationwide.

There is still more work to do and Lorenzo Herrera y Lozano with Kórima Press is getting it done when he and Alonzo agree to publish *Jotos Del Barrio* as a full length manuscript. Now, we can have the transformative work of Alonzo at our bedside (pun intended). In his final manuscript, the playwright sketches each character and scene with a text that reads like the detail in a fine-lined lithograph. The oppressed, silenced, afraid, celebrated, sexy, cerebral and spiritual joto identities intersect beyond the span of the three generations, and beyond the seriousness of each character's coming-out story throughout the narrative. His use of satire and double-entendre to awaken necessary comic relief gives the reader a place to join in the humor and learn to reclaim and rename the scars we carry. Alonzo even includes the screened *Straight on Queers* infomercials, which speak hilariously even on the page, "You see, mi gente, we at Jotas Concientizadas, Inc. consulted with the world's leading joto experts and quick-mouthed divas to put this video together....The result is this four hour video, guaranteed to turn you into a fast-tongued, quick thinking, all-knowing jota concientizada!" (Act II, Scene 7) In a humorous homage to the queer theorists, academics and creative scholars doing the work in our universities and communities throughout the world today, Alonzo introduces Dr. Tomás P. Ne, Ph.D., Jota Studies Expert who claims, "Having worked closely with Jotas Concientizadas, Inc., I too became a stronger willed, quick-minded, sharp-tongued queena." (Act II, Scene 7) Even in his humor, we are stirred and empowered. On the page, his words speak another language that goes beyond English or Spanish. On the pages of *Jotos del Barrio*, Alonzo's words speak joto, a language of el joto en el barrio, a story only we can tell, a story that does not retreat into the dark corner of the theater, the inside pockets of a suitcase, or at the bottom of a well made vodka cosmo. Jesús Alonzo's Joto resurrects from the humiliation of homophobia, as the "queen of the butterflies," earning her name because with her lightweight, delicate wings, the monarch escapes danger at all costs on her way to and from home, her barrio. And, "The metamorphosis begins here" in *Jotos del Barrio*. "Full thrust forward, / We stand on ground zero. We are blue, green, red, / copper, gold, and silver; / We are out and about / And without shame. // Sin vergüenza / So we will write." (Metamorphosis, Act II, Scene 11)

And, we will write. And, we will transform. And, we will soar into a barrio near you.

Gracias, mi querido joto.

Con Amor,

Anel I. Flores
May 16, 2014
San Antonio, Texas

Acknowledgements

Mil gracias to all the kings and queens of this jester's royally rasquache court:

To the madrinas of this book, the brilliant, Mr. Lorenzo Herrera y Lozano and the divinely divine, Mr. Dino Foxx;

To my cosmic twin, Anel I. Flores who is my soul-sister, my rock and my guide in many things life, but was especially that and so much more throughout the process of birthing this baby;

To Graciela I. Sánchez and the buenísima gente of the Esperanza Peace and Justice Center who first gave my work a home;

A mi linda mamacita, Aurora Alonzo, que no es nada rasquache, pero que siempre apoya todas mis travesuras rasquachistas;

To Emilio Morales Jr., my beloved partner in life and love, mi muy amado, mero-mero;

A mi hermano, Juan José Alonzo, who first inspired me to write;

To my great friends and mentors, Rolando Juárez, Yvonne M. Hernández, and Kristy Montemayor — I can only aspire to be as great as you someday;

To Kenneth Rainbolt, my dear friend and my dichotomous brother in life who on the one hand is my partner in all things bullshit and on the other is my most fearless and trusted ally;

To Agosto Cuellar, Alicia Fernandez (*In Memoriam*), and Franco Ontiveros, (*In Memoriam*) who supported my work from the very start;

To Ricardo Muñoz because even a heart attack could not stop him from leaving his mark on this play;

To the casts and crews of the 1995 reading, and the 2002 and 2014 productions of *Jotos del Barrio*, for their tireless work and commitment in making this work come alive;

To our Jot@ allies who support and love us unconditionally;

Y a tod@s l@s jot@s del barrio y del mundo entero, thank you for sharing your stories – our stories – and thank you for supporting my work.

Production Notes

Jotos del Barrio was originally written as a response piece to a Queer Media Studies class at Carleton College (Northfield, MN) in 1995. In the summer of that same year *Jotos del Barrio* was presented as a reading at the Esperanza Peace and Justice Center in San Antonio, TX. In the Spring of 2002, *Jotos del Barrio* was presented as a full scaled production at the Jump-Start Performance Co. in San Antonio, TX, where it set longstanding audience attendance records and later that summer received an extended run at the Esperanza Peace and Justice Center.

Jotos del Barrio

Act I

SCENE 1

Shh!

SPEAKER 1

(Stands up from among the audience.) Shh!

(Begins to make his way to the stage.) Don't let anyone know that you saw me here tonight. Dim the lights! I said dim the lights, damn it!

(Nervously.) No one should ever know I was here, at this performance. And no one should know that you're here either. If I were you I'd also be getting my things ready to leave, you know, right now, ri-right now before the show gets started and they bring up all the lights and everyone can see you.

(Short pause.) Don't you know how dangerous it is to be seen here, at this play? People might think you're a joto! Oh, sorry ma'am. Or they may think that you're a fag hag!

(Suddenly realizing.) Oh shit! Oh shit! I know you, don't I? Yeah, I do. Uh...uh...hi...uh...

(Suddenly.) Oh wait a minute, you're just another bar fly! What the hell are you doing here? This isn't a gay bar! We can't be jotitos here. This is a theatre for God's sake!

(Short pause, then realizing.) Oh great! Just great! There are more of us here, aren't there? Guys, you know we're not supposed to be gay outside our bars! Seriously, look around. How many openly queer public spaces do you know in this town besides the gay bars? Sure, there's a couple of spaces for us, but they are few and far between when compared to the gay bars. It's like we're only jotos when we drink. It just comes out with the alcohol! Instead of asking the bartender for a bottle of beer, you'd think we're asking him for a bottle of queer! I know the state finally repealed its sodomy laws but that didn't change much. We are still considered by many to be sexual outlaws; and our allies are treated as our sexual accomplices. They are berated with insults — immoral radicals, closet case leftists, wanton sinners, they are called — simply for supporting us, simply for loving their fellow human beings.

(Concerned.) You think we're safe in here? I hope so. No one will come get us in here. I mean it's not like we're in the days of the Holy Inquisition. They can no longer kill us for being jotos, right? Man, if you were even suspected of jotería in those days the Church and State burned you at the stake or simply tore you apart, literally. They tied your limbs to four different horses and quartered you. Your arms went one way, your legs went another, and your heart and soul went exactly where the Church and State told them to go!

(SPEAKER 2 stands up from the audience and makes his way to the stage.)

SPEAKERS 1 & 2
But shh!

SPEAKER 1
We're not supposed to know that savages governed us. Some of them attained saintly status and still others are the great heroes we learn about in our textbooks. That's all over now; so we are told, but have you ever heard of hate crimes? You know, when someone gets physically or verbally assaulted simply for being a woman, or transgender, or for being of a non-White race, or for being homosexual. You know why they're called hate crimes, right?

SPEAKERS 1 & 2
Shh!

SPEAKER 2
I'll tell you. They're called hate crimes because the law hates to investigate them, the law hates to report them, and the law hates to acknowledge that they occur everyday because the law hates to accept that people who are not White, heterosexual males are also human beings worthy of the same human rights as everyone else. What we demand are not special privileges, damn it! Oh the government pretends that they are protecting us against acts of violence, but don't be fooled. The government only calls them hate crimes to protect itself from the very hate its own institutions provoke! It's another case of mislabeling the real issue; kind of like with biological terrorism. We are told it all has to do with the use of biological matter,

JESÚS ALONZO

such as anthrax and smallpox, in acts of terrorism. But that's something else. If you ask me, a better name for that type of warfare might be the Thirdworldization of America. And let me tell you, child, it is terrorizing!

(Short pause then to audience.) You don't know what I'm talking about? Well then I invite you to visit any third world country to see the astounding number of people — in particular, children — who are dying or living with life threatening illnesses as a result of exposure to murderous biological matter. Smallpox, AIDS, dysentery, polio, famine; these aren't so rare in Central and South America, or Africa and Southeast Asia. Money, healthcare, food, and access to potable drinking water on the other hand, can be about as rare as the fucking Chupacabra!

(Laughing.) Biological terrorism? I'll tell you what that really is.

(SPEAKER 3 stands up from the audience and makes his way to the stage.)

SPEAKERS 1, 2, & 3
Shh!

SPEAKER 3
It is racism, sexism, and homophobia. It is the persecution of peoples who are biologically something other than White, heterosexual males. And unless you experience living life as something other than a White, heterosexual male you may never know what it means to truly fear and survive biological terror. From the inception of our country's history to the present, non-White, heterosexual male citizens are continuously terrorized based solely on their bio-molecular structures. But, shh, we're not supposed to know that either. And if we do, we're supposed to ignore it.

(Suddenly realizing.) Oh God, look at the time. The show is about to get started and I'm still here talking. Remember! Don't tell anyone that you saw me here, please.

(Speaker 4 stands up from the audience and makes his way to the stage.)

ALL

Shh!

SPEAKER 4

No one should know of my presence here tonight. I'll tell you why.
I'll confess, but only if you promise to deny that you ever saw me here.
I'm...I'm...

SPEAKER 1

I'm a teacher.

SPEAKER 2

I work retail.

SPEAKER 3

I'm a United States Army sergeant.

SPEAKER 4

I take care of the elderly.

SPEAKER 2

I'm a part-time student and full-time community organizer.

SPEAKER 1

I'm a construction site project manager.

SPEAKER 4

I'm an entrepreneur.

SPEAKER 3

I'm a bank teller.

ALL

I am you.

SPEAKER 4

... a proud, hardworking, tax-paying member of the American workforce. I admit, sometimes my work is hard but I enjoy what I do and I relish in knowing that I am this country's backbone. What I don't enjoy...

SPEAKER 3

What I don't enjoy...

SPEAKER 1

What I don't enjoy...

SPEAKER 2

What I don't enjoy...

SPEAKER 4

...is checking my bags in at the door.

ALL

Everyday!

SPEAKER 3

Everyday, I check-in two suitcases. One is neatly packed con el barrio that I grew up in, my two working class parents who speak only Spanish, my father's pasado as a mojado, los frijolitos del jarro y las tortillitas caseras.

(Aside.) They are not so lucrative in the professional world, you know.

SPEAKER 2

I also packed all the hand-me-down clothes that my older siblings so lovingly sacrificed for me as we grew up, and the handmade huaraches my parents bought me across the border.

SPEAKER 1

Cornelio Reyna, Ramón Ayala, Lucha Villa, Lola Beltrán, Selena, Mingo Saldivar, and Tony de la Rosa, along with my papa's gritos are all packed in here too.

SPEAKER 4

And to maintain order and keep the peace, I packed in César Chávez, my indio ancestors, my curandera grandmother, Juan Diego y la Virgen. This is the first suitcase I check-in.

SPEAKER 3

In the other suitcase, I packed the desires of a man who loves men, all the men I can't remember and those I can't forget. The secret compartment of this suitcase tenderly stows the experiences of my first true love. In its inside liners you can find all the gay bars and clubs, their patrons and drag shows, the catty catcalls, and the leather nights where almost no one is dressed in leather. The memories of Olmos Park on Sundays; the cruisy trails of McAllister Park and Acequia Park over by the old missions; the Esperanza Peace and Justice Center and the Jump-Start Theatre along with other openly queer friendly spaces also fill the liners of this suitcase. In the outside pockets, I stuffed all the hurtful names and judgments passed upon me along with all the fears I ever experienced.

SPEAKER 2

All my dirty magazines and videos, all my books on queer theory, all the literature I read, and all the literature I wrote, fill this suitcase too.

SPEAKER 1

Together these things are all neatly packed into two separate suitcases that, when opened, merge into one singular existence. And it is this existence — my existence — that I must check-in at the door everyday because if I want to be fully integrated into our great American society I must forget who I am and allow myself to remember only on those designated dates, weeks, or months. And when I do acknowledge myself, my celebrations should be superficial and all-inclusive, lest I be labeled an elitist racist heterophobe. Yes, if it is my desire to be acknowledged as a full citizen of this country, I must uphold the morals and values of White, middle-class America.

(He freezes. A white light shines from above him as the stage lights dim. The chorus of the Hallelujah Chorus plays. When it ends, the scene resumes.)

JESÚS ALONZO

ALL

My livelihood depends on it!

SPEAKER 4

Therefore, I play servant to a system that will never accept or embrace me for all that I truly am.

SPEAKER 2

But you do not need to have a lucrative position at work to play this game.

SPEAKER 3

You don't even need to be a professional to do what I do. I know that many of us, that many of you also check your bags in at the door.

ALL

Everyday!

SPEAKER 3

Perhaps you do this for fear of being persecuted or perhaps you do it for fear of being fired.

SPEAKER 2

Or maybe you just don't want to be you.

SPEAKER 4

Whatever the case, we have all done it at some point!

SPEAKER 1

So let's cut a deal. You don't tell anyone that you saw me here tonight, and I won't tell anyone that I saw you here tonight.

ALL

Shh!

(BLACKOUT)

(END OF SCENE)

Scene 2

Metamorfosis

(The ORATOR moves to the beat of the spoken word as multicolored lights illuminate the stage. He is dressed in white and is barefooted.)

It begins in a verse:
a poem that will be
sung. A
song that will be
danced. A
dance that will
end.
And such is life,
or this one at least.

The metamorphosis
Begins here.

A new man?
—perhaps,
but not really.

The new man who comes out
is the same, same one
who once hid inside a frail boy.
But now he is out
and about
and without shame.
Sin vergüenza.

Full thrust forward,
he stands on ground zero.
He is blue, green, red,
copper, gold, and silver;
Answers yes to the word
man.

Answers yes to the word
Xicano.
Answers yes to the word
gay.

Gay Xicano Man:
The metamorphosis
has begun—
The metamorphosis
will continue.

Gay Xicano Man
dances.
Gay Xicano Man
sings.
Gay Xicano Man
writes
the poems that turn into the
verses
he loves to dance and sing.

(BLACKOUT)

(END OF SCENE)

Scene 3

Straight on Queers Infomercial:
Video Installment #1

(The video opens to a middle-aged man standing on the set of a television studio. He is casually dressed in slacks, a dress shirt, and a sport coat. To his left sits a display of the video, *Straight On Queers*.)

HOST

(Speaking directly into the camera.) Are you ever left speechless because of someone else's ignorant statements? Well if you're a joto, perhaps you know what I'm talking about. How many times do people speak to you, pleasantly, without meaning any harm and then suddenly, BAM!, they punch you across the face with an unintended slur of ignorance?

(Laughs to himself.) I know you know what I'm talking about. Allow me to demonstrate. How many times have these remarks slammed you?

(The scene changes to a woman on the street. She wears large sunglasses and vintage clothing. She chews gum loudly as she speaks directly into the camera.)

BYSTANDER #1

You like men? Well, okay, I guess. I mean, well, like if God wanted you to be a woman, you would've like, well, been born a girl, you understand?

(The scene cuts back to HOST.)

HOST

Or how about this little number?

(The scene changes to a football player coming off the playing field. He takes his helmet off as he runs to the camera. He stops and looks directly into it as he speaks.)

JESÚS ALONZO

BYSTANDER #2

You know, I would never guess that you are a gay!

(Licks his lips hungrily, almost suggestively.) I mean you don't look like a fag!

(The scene cuts back to HOST.)

HOST

Whoa! How many times have you heard that one? Pues if you are as tired as I am of these and so many other ignorant statements about jotos, have I got the video for you! And no, it is not a porn flick. It's not even a boring instructional video. In fact, boring, is the last adjective used to describe this intriguing piece. And what a piece it is!

(Reaches for a video from display.) Introducing the one and only video that will turn you into a fast tongued, quick thinking, all-knowing jota conscientizada: *Straight on Queers!*

(There is a full-screen flash of the video box.)

And today, as an introductory offer, we bring it to you for the low, low price of only $19.95!

(Aside.) Plus shipping and handling. And if you ask me, that's a little money for such a huge investment.

(Suddenly serious.) Through this video you will not only learn how to find your voice in this world of heterosexual dominance, but you will also learn how to respond proactively to the many ignorant and biased slanders against you as a joto. I know it's changed my life! Find it hard to believe? Well let's revisit our first scenario.

(The video replays BYSTANDER #1's statement.)

BYSTANDER #1

You like men? Well, okay, I guess. I mean, well, like if God wanted you to be a woman, you would've like, well, been born a girl, you understand?

JOTO #1

(He is a young Latino in his mid-twenties and he is dressed casually. He stares helplessly into the camera, not knowing how to respond.)

Uh, I...uh, I...I guess?

(The scene cuts back to HOST.)

HOST

¡No! ¡Dios mío! That is no way to respond. This boy is in serious need of a little education, not to mention a quick tongue. But where can he find them?

(Short pause.) Thank goodness for *Straight on Queers!* Had this young man watched our video before his conversation, I guarantee that instead of standing in a state of mental shock, he would be delivering a shock to this lady's mental state! Watcha this!

(Video scene cuts back to the street scene and JOTO #1.)

JOTO #1

(Feisty now.) You are absolutely right, mi amor. If God wanted me to be a woman, I would've been born a girl or perhaps even a male-to-female transgender. But I was not. By the same token, if God wanted me to be straight or bisexual, I would've been born liking women. But I was not. I was born liking, no, excuse me, loving, exclusively loving men. So I guess God must've wanted me to be a homosexual! Understand?

(VIDEO OUT)

(END OF SCENE)

JESÚS ALONZO

Scene 4

Mamá, soy homosexual

(At rise, SON is watching MOTHER, who is at home in her own world. MOTHER holds a picture of SON and looks onto it fondly. SON speaks toward MOTHER, though she cannot see or hear him. By the poem's end, SON is crouching and holds himself in a fetal position.)

So she speaks only Spanish
Nada más
Ni una gota de inglés
And I must confess to her,
"Mommy, I'm gay"
Pero no hay palabras

I can say,
"Mamá, soy homosexual,"
Because it's the right word to say
The correct word to describe
Who I am
But Spanish or English
The word homosexual
Emphasis on sex
Never appealed
To my liking
And so I think, and think again of some other words
To express the who, what, and how that I am
But for as much as I think
I cannot help but
Damn my native tongue, Spanish
And as much as I love it
I am altogether revolted by it
Because the only other words to choose from
Are not just words,
But hateful insults

I can say,
"Mamá, soy marica, maricón,
joto, chifladito, curiosito,
invertido, un sodomita,
un ninfo, un perverso, un putito,
una loca, una vieja
—usted sabe,
uno de aquellos"

Pero no
I am not one of those
As these insults tell me
I am not about gender confusion
Or sexual perversions
Or dehumanizing
Or demoralizing myself
As these insults imply
There's much more to me than same-gender sex
In fact,
I am still a part of humanity

But how do I tell my mama
How do I make her comprehend
That I am gay,
And still human,
Still the boy she raised to be a man

How do I tell my mama
Who speaks only Spanish
How do I make her comprehend
Que yo no soy de amor entre hombre y mujer…

…Homosexual,
¡Que pinche palabra!

JESÚS ALONZO

Mi'jo

(After a pause from the previous poem, MOTHER puts down the picture of SON. She acknowledges his presence and speaks to him. He remains in a dreamlike state. Her movements are choreographed so that by the poem's end MOTHER holds SON as Mary holds Jesus in Michelangelo's Pietà.)

Mi'jo
Ya un hombre grande y maduro
Independiente y educado
Hoy preguntas
Si a un hijo homosexual
Puedo yo amar

Esta es mi respuesta

Por nueve meses de mi vida
Mi'jo
Te cargué dentro mi cuerpo
Por nueve meses
Mi'jo
Fuimos un sólo ser
Tú y yo
Un sólo ser

Cuántas fueron las horas
Mi'jo
Que al darte luz
Acostada pasé
Con el corazón abierto
Llorando y sudando
Rogándole a Dios
Y a la Virgencita
Que todo pasara pronto
Que todo saliera bien

Ay qué dolor eterno pasé
Pero nunca con este dolor sufrí
Porque fue allí
Que yo aprendí
A amarte eternamente

Y al nacer
Mi'jo
La sangre que cubría tu cuerpo
Era sangre de mi corazón
Y fue con esta sangre pura y fina que yo te bañé
Porque eras mío, mío
Mi hijo, mío
Quien me causó el más supremo
Dolor de amor

Es por eso
Hijo mío
Que mi respuesta
A tu pregunta es
Sí
Seas lo que seas
Hagas lo que hagas
Eternamente te amaré

(BLACKOUT)

(END OF SCENE)

JESÚS ALONZO

Scene 5

Tony's Mother's Car

(At rise, TONY stands front, center stage with only a spotlight on him.)

TONY

I had no problem being at home and in the closet. As far as I was concerned, my family would never know of the double life I led: straight, closeted college boy by day and raging queer club kid por la noche. They had no clue about me! My parents couldn't even begin to fathom that their little mi'jito was un jotinchón de primera. I didn't know how they would react if I told them. What if they threw me out of the house or worse yet, disowned me? For as long as I was living at home, I needed to remember the words of my papacito lindo.

(Light comes up middle stage left to reveal FATHER.)

FATHER

Mi'jito, necesitas aprender a ser macho. ¡Necesitas ser puro hombre, mi'jo!

(Light comes up middle stage right to reveal MOTHER.)

MOTHER

Sí, mi'jito, hazle caso a tu padre. ¡Mi hombrecito chulo!

(Lights go out on FATHER and MOTHER.)

TONY

Everything was going well with my little covert operation. My joto-self was completely concealed from my parents. But then came that fateful Saturday night when all shit hit the fan and the cat was let out of the bag, or should I say, the jotito out of his armoire? You see, my old carcacha was broken down; man I had no way to get around. And you know there was no way I could stay home and miss a Saturday night out at the club. That's what I lived for! I was young, good looking, and, mmm, I was always lookin' fly.

TONY (Continued.)

I just couldn't resist! I was not staying home. So I asked my mom if I could borrow her car that night. Man, as soon as she said,

MOTHER

(Off stage.) ¡Claro, mi rey!

TONY

I was off to the club for another eventful night out —and that it was!

(TONY walks off stage right. Multicolored lights flash throughout the stage and dance music plays to create the feel of a night club. LUIS and several other young men enter the stage and begin to dance. TONY reenters, stage left. He wears black leather pants and boots with a form-fitting Versace button-down shirt. He waves at LUIS who abandons the dance floor to approach his friend. The others exit as the music fades.)

S'up, fool! Lookin' tight, papi chulo! Get over here and lemme get a piece of that!

(The two friends embrace and give each other a friendly kiss.)

LUIS

(Still holding TONY in his arms.) ¿Que pasó, Tony? I wasn't expecting to see you tonight.

(Releasing their embrace.) I thought your car was in the shop, mentiroso.

TONY

Nah, Luis, it is in the shop. I borrowed my ma's car at the last minute.

LUIS

I was gonna say. Maybe you just didn't wanna give me a ride tonight.

TONY

C'mon, Luis, you know I wouldn't play my best girl like that. I love you, man.

JESÚS ALONZO

LUIS

Back at you, cabrón.

(Suddenly.) ¡Epa! You look damn good! Check you out with your leather pants, your tight-ass boots, and, mmm, that shirt just hugs you in all the right places. ¡Cabrón! What is that anyways?

TONY

(Bragging.) ¡Pues Versace, buey!

LUIS

Of course!

TONY

Of course!

LUIS

You look like a million bucks, fool. (Half whispering.) Check out smiley over there! He's had his eye on you since you walked in. You should go talk to him.

TONY

Oh, c'mon, Luis. He ain't even my type. (Looks around, then suddenly.) Hey, check out that one over there. Now that's fine!

LUIS

That queen? Please! Don't tell me you like that!

TONY

Which one?

LUIS

(Pointing with his chin.) Pues that one! La gorda in the red muscle shirt and Missions baseball cap.

TONY

Her? Oh hell no! She all caps U-G-L-Y! I was talking about the vaquero behind her, the one in the white jeans. (Excited.) Check 'em out, he's turning towards us.

LUIS

(Surprised.) Oh, da-amn!

TONY

I know, dude!

LUIS

Now that's what I call a showstopper!

TONY

Whatever! I mean, he's cute, but he ain't no Adonis!

LUIS

Dude, I was talking about his package!

TONY

Oh. (Suddenly realizing.) Oh! Da-amn! Holy cock, buttman!

LUIS

Amen to that, honey! (Giddy.) Tony, he's coming over here.

BARTENDER

(Off stage.) Last call!

TONY

C'mon girl, let's get outta here. I need a strong drink to get over what I just saw!

(TONY pulls LUIS away to stage right.)

LUIS

(Disappointed.) Ah, c'mon Tony! Ain't nothing wrong with a little tease.

TONY

Yeah, but I don't wanna get teased by that. You saw the monster he was packing! Scary!

LUIS

But I bet it feels nice in all the right spots!

TONY

You're such a size queen!

LUIS

Tony, you know that's not all that matters to me! (Aside.) But it sure is a nice incentive.

TONY

Of course you'd say that!

LUIS

Of course!

TONY

(Looks back.) Oh good, he's gone.

LUIS

(Looking around and noticing.) Check it out, Tony. I guess it's just you and me. Those other cabrones left without even telling us goodbye.

TONY

¡Qué gacho! ¿Y ahora? How are you getting home, bro? (Laughing.) You know the bus stopped running three hours ago.

LUIS

Pues I guess…you!

TONY

(Laughing.) Should've known!

TONY (Continued.)

(LUIS freezes. The flashing lights stop and dim lights come up. TONY addresses the audience anew. He crosses to front stage left as he speaks.)

We took our last shot for the night and danced it off with a couple more songs. At about three in the morning, we were finally ready to leave. I mean, our friends were all gone, and God knows we really didn't meet anyone worth sticking around for. So there really was no other reason for us to stay. As we headed to the parking lot, Luis asked,

LUIS

(Unfreezes and comes up to TONY.) Hey cabrón, where'd you park, anyway?

TONY

(To audience.) As I looked around trying to find my mom's car, I thought, "Damn, that's a good question." The parking lot was almost empty. It didn't make sense not to find my mom's car. And besides, I remember exactly where I parked it. But I stayed open to the possibility that maybe I somehow forgot.

(Pauses to look around.) After looking around some more, and after convincing myself that the car just wasn't where I knew I parked it, I realized that it was gone!

(Suddenly to LUIS, panicking.) ¡En la pinche madre, Luis! My ma's car got stolen! What the hell am I gonna do? Hurry man, think of someone we can call to give us a ride. I can't let my parents know where the car got stolen!

LUIS

Hey Tony, you know que aquellos aren't even home yet. ¡Son bien tragones! They probably stopped by to throw down a munch at Mr. Taco.

(Takes a short pause to swallow.) Besides man, we gotta call the cops to report the car stolen. Y, ¡pues hijo! man, the cops gotta know where the car got stolen from.

TONY

Shit! I guess there's no way around this one, huh?

(LUIS nods his head in agreement.)

Let me check out your cell phone, bro. I promise I won't be long.

LUIS

(Handing TONY his cell phone.) It's cool, girl, take your time. I got weekend minutes.

TONY

(To audience.) Slowly and nervously, I dialed my parent's phone number.

(TONY pauses as he begins to cross to center stage. LUIS follows close behind.)

First ring...second ring...third ring...

(Lights come up middle stage right to reveal the kitchen where FATHER stands shirtless in his pajamas, answering the phone.)

FATHER

(Waking up.) ¿B-b-b-bueno?

(MOTHER enters kitchen in her nightgown, also waking up.)

TONY

(Nervously.) He-he-hello, ¿apá?

FATHER

¿Qui-quién habla?

TONY

Soy yo, apá, Tony. I ah, ah...

FATHER

(Suddenly awake.) ¿Qué pasó, Antonio? ¿Estás bien? Where are you?

MOTHER

(Alarmed.) ¿Qué pasó con Toñito, viejo?

FATHER

Shh! Hold on, mujer!

TONY

Sí, apá, I'm fine, but I got some bad news. (Short pause.) Ah, apá? Hello, are you still there? ¿Apá?

FATHER

Of course I'm still here, cabrón! Where'd you expect me to go?

TONY

Oh, hi, apá …

FATHER

(Interrupting.) ¡Con una chingada, Antonio! What happened?

TONY

Oh, perdón. I thought maybe you hung up. Ah, apá, ma's car was…ah…ah…Apá, ma's car got stolen from the parking lot where I parked it.

FATHER

¿Cómo que your mother's car got stolen?

MOTHER

¡Ay! ¡No me digas que se robaron mi carrito!

FATHER

(To MOTHER.) Calm down, hombre!

TONY

I'm trying to stay calm, apá. It's just that…

FATHER

(Interrupting TONY.) Not you, muchacho! I'm talking to your mother!

(Short pause.) Did you lock the car, Antonio? You probably left the keys in the ignition, ¿no?

TONY

No apá, I locked it. And I have the keys here with me. I guess someone broke into it.

FATHER

¡Ay, Antonio! Are you sure? Maybe you parked it somewhere else.

TONY

No, I already checked everywhere and I didn't find it.

(Short pause.) My friend Luis and I need a ride a home.

FATHER

And did you call the police?

MOTHER

¡La policía! ¡Hay, por el amor de Dios!

(Frustrated.) ¿Pues qué chingados pasó?

FATHER

¡Ahorita te digo, mujer!

TONY

Ah, no, apá, I haven't called the police.

FATHER

¿Pues what are you waiting for, muchacho? ¡Llámales! Now where'd you say you're at?

(Lights come down on FATHER and MOTHER.)

TONY

(To audience.) I gave him directions to the club and hung up. Then I called the cops. What else could I do?

(Short pause.) En un ratito my mind took off on me. What was I going to tell my parents when they found out I was at a gay club? I started thinking that maybe they didn't need to know. But then, what if the cops asked?

(Short pause.) I guess I could lie to them, right?

(Short pause.) But then, what would I tell them?

(Short pause.) Shit, shit, shit!

(TONY pauses to look behind him. He realizes a police officer entering from back stage left and his parents entering from back stage right, simultaneously.)

A little while later the cops and my parents got there, dude, at the same time, almost like they planned it! And Luis and I were just shitting bricks!

COP

(Speaking with a thick American accent.) Bueno, bueno, bueno, let's see, who's the owner of the allegedly stolen vehicle?

MOTHER

Yo, señor policía.

COP

¿Usted? Bueno, okay.

TONY

But I was driving it before it got stolen.

COP

And your name is?

(Short pause, then suddenly.) Tu nombre, por favor.

TONY

Antonio Juárez.

LUIS

(Aside.) He understood you the first time.

COP

(To LUIS.) Excuse me? ¿Perdón?

LUIS

(Imitating COP'S accent.) No, nada, señor policía.

COP

(Disregarding LUIS.) And your name, ma'am?

MOTHER

Guadalupe Juárez.

FATHER

(Handing COP some documents.) Here's a copy of the car's title, license and insurance card.

COP

(Reviews documents indifferently.) Wow, you actually have insurance. Que bien. Muchos gracias.

(To TONY.) Now, Antonio, did you happen to leave the keys in the car?

(Pantomiming with hand.) ¿La llaves?

TONY

No, I got the keys right here with me.

COP

All right, then.

(Still pantomiming each question.) What about the doors? ¿Las puertas? Did you lock them? Were the windows rolled all the way up? ¿Para arriba?

TONY

As far as I know and as far as I can remember, yeah. And just so you know, we can all speak and understand English here, man.

COP

It's sir to you, son! ¿Comprende?

TONY

Excuse me, sir.

COP

(To himself, reviewing his report.) Okay now, let's see. The doors were rolled all the way up, the windows were locked; got the title, license plates, the insurance card but I still need to verify it's real, and...

(Then suddenly.) ...ah, yes! Antonio, por favor, can you please tell me exactly where you were between the time you left the car and the time you realized the care was gone?

TONY

(To audience.) Of all the God-forsaken questions to ask me, he had to ask that one? Until now, my parents had no idea that we were standing in the parking lot of a gay club. But now the moment of truth arrived. Nervously, I pointed in the direction of the club.

(To COP, pointing.) Over there, sir.

COP

¿Dónde, Antonio? Over there? Inside that club? ¿En ese antro?

TONY

Yes sir.

LUIS

(Frustrated, still imitating COP.) ¡Sí, en ese antro!

JESÚS ALONZO

COP

(Aggressively to LUIS.) I am talking to your amiga!

(Back to TONY, inquisitively.) Now, Antonio, do you frequent that club?

TONY

(Nervously.) Excuse me?

COP

Are you a regular patron of that establishment?

(Trying to explain himself.) Uh, how often do you go to that club, son?

TONY

Oh! Uh...uh...wait, I'm not sure what that has to do with my mom's car being stolen.

COP

Son, when an authority asks you a question, you answer that question. ¿Entendido?

(Short pause.) Now, how often do you go to that club?

TONY

(Defeated.) Just about every Saturday, sir.

COP

(Writing in his report.) Hmm, I see. Who would've guessed it?

(Takes a deep breath as he speaks.) Ah, estos pinches maricones...

MOTHER

¿Que-qué?

(MOTHER charges at COP while FATHER attempts to hold her back.)

¡Óigame no, viejo jodido. Más respeto, por favor!

MOTHER (Continued.)

(Calming down, to FATHER.) Es que primero nos manda el idioma a la chingada y luego nos insulta a nuestro hijo. ¡Óyeme, no!

(Back to COP.) What porquerías are you talking about, señor policía?

COP

No nada, nada, señora, cálmese. But por favor comprende that if your hija was not inside that club for homosexuales, you might still have your carro.

LUIS

(Aside.) ¡Pinche puerco marrano! ¡Bestia!

TONY

(To audience.) And with that, he sealed the deal! ¡Me dio en la mera chota, el buey! I stood there trying to smile. I looked straight at the ground; the whole time I was yelling inside myself, '¡Trágame tierra!' I wanted to disappear, but nothing happened. I just stood there, feeling myself shrinking under my parents' eyes. I glanced at Luis, and I could tell he felt the same way.

(Short pause.) After what seemed like hours of silence, my pa finally said,

FATHER

¿Ya es todo, señor policía?

COP

Sí, señor. We'll give you a call as soon as we locate your carro, that is, (Chuckling.) if we locate it, of course.

LUIS

Of course!

(Imitating COP.) ¡Claro!

FATHER

(To LUIS.) Okay, okay, ¡ya basta!

FATHER (Continued.)

(FATHER extends his arm to shake the COP'S hand.) Muchas gracias.

(COP looks at FATHER'S hand and disregards the gesture as he exits.)

(To himself and gesturing.) Pues chinga tu madre, cabrón!

(Back to others.) Everybody, get in the car.

(FATHER, MOTHER, TONY, and LUIS mimic riding in a car. FATHER is driving, MOTHER sits in the front passenger seat, and TONY and LUIS sit in the back. There is a pause as they begin to drive. Everyone appears very uncomfortable. FATHER takes in deep breaths repeatedly, MOTHER holds her tears back, and TONY and LUIS continuously exchange glances.)

TONY

(Whispering to LUIS.) Dude, this is so fucked up; of all the cars to steal...

LUIS

(Serious.) Be quiet, man, this ain't the time...

(TONY nods his head in agreement and continues the silent, uncomfortable ride. After a short pause, they mimic a stop where LUIS gets off the car and exits the stage. After another short pause they mimic their arrival and all exit the car. MOTHER and FATHER cross to stage right where they sit at the kitchen table.)

TONY

(To audience as he crosses to the kitchen to join parents.) We got inside and went straight to the kitchen. I just stood there in complete silence.

(TONY stands between his parents who sit there, pensively.) I kept psyching myself out that they were feeling like this because of the car.

(Short pause.) Nah. I was wrong. They were definitely feeling this way because of me.

TONY (Continued.)

(To parents.) Look, I know what you're thinking and I can tell that you're pissed off...

FATHER

Watch you mouth in front of your mother, ¡con una chingada!

TONY

Perdón. I'm sorry, amá.

MOTHER

No, don't worry about it, mi'jo.

(Turning to FATHER.) I've heard worse before.

TONY

But like I was telling you, I know that you're wondering why I was at that gay club. Well...the truth is that's where I hang out on Saturday nights.

MOTHER

But, mi'jo, why if that place is for...for...¡ay, para aquella gente...los homosexuales! ¡Ay, Dios me libre!

TONY

Exactly, amá. Por favor, I know it might be hard, but I want you to understand that...that...

(Takes a deep breath.) I want you to understand that I go to that club because I'm also a homosexual.

MOTHER

Ay, don't say it that way!

TONY

(Respectfully.) How else do you want me to say it, amá? I can't sugarcoat it for you. I'm gay. I am a homosexual. Okay?

TONY (Continued.)

(Short pause then to audience.) Holy shit! I actually just said it. I actually told my parents that I was gay! It was like the weight of the world suddenly coming off my shoulders! ¡Órale!

FATHER

No, pues...pues if you say so, ¿qué le vamos a hacer?

TONY

¿Amá?

MOTHER

No, pues, whatever your dad says, mi'jo.

TONY

No, amá. I want to know what you have to say. Mira, if this upsets you so much, I'll leave this minute and I will try to never bother our family again.

MOTHER

¡No, mi'jo! This is your house. You have no need to go anywhere else.

(Pleading.) But please, mi'jo, have some patience with me. I...I don't even know what to say. What do you want me to say?

TONY

You tell me what you want. Tell me what's in your heart, amá. Just tell me what you think. Por favor.

MOTHER

Antonio, tú eres mi hijo, and not anyone nor anything can ever change that; but for as much as I want to, mi'jo, no entiendo...

FATHER

(Interrupting.) No pues who's going to understand that? ¡Me imagino que ni el pinche diablo lo entiende!

MOTHER

(To Father.) ¡Joaquín Alejandro, ya para con esa boca, por favor! ¡No me pierdas el respeto porque no te doy lugar! ¿Me oíste? Menos mal.

(Back to Tony.) Antonio, no sé. I feel so guilty, as if it's all my fault. What did I do wrong?

TONY

¡Ay, amá, por favor! It's no one's fault that I am gay. Y además, you always did the best for me and gave me the best you could…

FATHER

(Interrupting again.) ¡Precisamente! Then why did you come out like this?

TONY

(Frustrated.) How, apá? You think I'm psychotic, like there's something clinically wrong with my head? Is that what you think? Because if it is, you need to know that who I am is not an illness.

FATHER

Then what happened with you?

TONY

What do you mean, "what happened with you?" Nothing! This is part of who I am.

(Short pause, searching.) A ver, my two brothers seem straight, and we grew up here in this same house. Why aren't you asking what happened with them?

FATHER

Because I already know that nothing happened with them!

TONY

¡Exactamente! Nothing happened with me either. Así soy, quiera quién lo quiera; le guste a quién le guste. I've known it since I was a little boy, apá.

MOTHER

(Defusing the situation.) Antonio, mira, give us some time to think things over. This is all so new to us. It's just that these kinds of things happen on Cristina, Don Francisco y hasta en la pinche Oprah! ¿Pero aquí, en mi propia casa, con mi propio hijo?

FATHER

Antonio, the thing is that in this family there's never been a maric...que diga, un, un gay, ¡hombre!

TONY

You mean there's never been one who admitted it, ¿no? Because my tío Chucho, no sé, pero a mí se me hace que anda por las mismas.

FATHER

¡Antonio!

TONY

I'm sorry, apá, but it's like you've always said, "no podemos tapar el sol con un dedo." We have to see things for what they are even if it's your baby brother or your own children that we're talking about.

FATHER

But you don't know that about your tío!

TONY

Apá, tío Chucho has never been married, he's never had a girlfriend that we know of, and he's always, and I mean always with his friend José.

FATHER

But they're just gym buddies, Antonio.

TONY

Apá, gym buddies spot each other in the weight room. Tío Chucho and José vacation together, spend Christmas and New Year's together, and they're always spending a night at each other's house! C'mon, dad, they even do each other's laundry!

FATHER

¡Ya basta, Antonio!

MOTHER

Pues whatever tío Chucho may or may not be, one thing's for sure, ese hombre makes an amazing cosmopolitan!

FATHER

(Suddenly realizing.) ¡Me lleva la chingada!

TONY

Okay, okay, apá. Calm down. I didn't mean to stir up any trouble.

(Backtracking.) Maybe tío Chucho is not gay. We don't know that for sure. But I am. I already admitted that to myself and now I'm admitting it to you. I love you. I need you to love me back.

MOTHER

This doesn't make me stop loving you, mi'jo! But like I told you, please give us time.

TONY

¿Apá?

FATHER

(Indifferently.) I gotta be real honest with you, son. Right now I'm a little bit more worried about your mother's car than anything else.

MOTHER

(Gives FATHER a sharp look then begins to stand.) Antonio, I want you to know that this will always be your casita and I am here to help you with whatever I can. También quiero que te cuides porque te quiero mucho, mi rey.

TONY

¿Y usted, apá?

JESÚS ALONZO

FATHER

(Still indifferent.) ¿Y yo qué?

TONY

Do you still love me?

FATHER

¿Pues no eres mi sangre?

MOTHER

(To FATHER.) ¡Ya! ¡No seas tan pinche y tan macho con tu hijo!

FATHER

(Stands up.) ¡Chingado! Antonio, you just unloaded this information on us. What am I supposed to say?

(Searching.) I just don't understand.

MOTHER

But that doesn't mean we're gonna close our doors on you or stop loving you.

FATHER

(Takes a deep breath, pensively.) No. ¿Cómo crees? Of course we're not gonna close our doors on our son.

(Short pause.) But like your mother says, give us some time. Let's just take this one day at a time. ¿Puede ser?

TONY

Of course, apá. I can understand it's difficult for you. It's hard for me, too.

FATHER

(Comes up to TONY and places a hand on his shoulder.) I know, son. But it's all good. It's good.

FATHER (Continued.)

(Turns to MOTHER and begins to lead her out of the kitchen.) Let's just get to bed now.

MOTHER

¿Sabes qué viejo? I'm going to invite tío Chucho and José over to the house next Friday.

FATHER

For what? To teach Antonio how to make a good cosmopolitan?

TONY

¡Apá!

FATHER

(To MOTHER.) I might as well take advantage of the benefits that come with having a gay son. ¿No?

TONY

That is such a stereotype, apá!

MOTHER

Your father is only joking with you, mi'jito.

FATHER

Anda, let's get to bed.

TONY

Okay, allí voy.

(Lights go out on kitchen as FATHER and MOTHER exit. The original spotlight comes up on TONY who crosses back to center stage speaking to audience.)

So that's how it went down that night. My secret was out. All we could do was face the truth and deal with it.

TONY (Continued.)

(Laughing to himself.) And we did, very slowly but definitely very surely. And do you want to know something? Everything turned out okay. I mean, my father still struggles with it and makes his little comments every now and then, but he's learning to correct himself. What can I say? He's a work in progress. I guess I can live with that. As for my brothers, well they swear that they always knew I was gay and were just waiting for me to come out. Go figure! But my true rock is my ma. She's just a badass mujer. After her car turned up in a ditch completely totaled, don't you know la Miss Ay Tú María Cantú went out and bought herself a brand new sports car! No kidding, man! And she made sure it came with one of those really annoying alarms that go off if you even look at the damn thing. She told me I could borrow it anytime I wanted, but I said, "no, thank you!" Hell, I learned my lesson and I will never borrow anyone's car again!

(Dance music comes on as multicolored lights begin to flash. TONY dances.)

(BLACKOUT)

(END OF SCENE)

Scene 6

Joto Macho

(JOTO MACHO, a vaquero, comes out dancing to Tejano music. JOTO MACHO speaks as the music fades.)

¡Imposible!
How could this be?
A man,
Un macho como yo,
¿Ser joto?

¿Pero cómo?

Un hombre
Tan hombre:
Tejanito
With my tight Wrangler jeans
My wide brimmed Stetson
y mis botas vaqueras

This chiseled barba,
This heavenly body
Estas nachas
And my deep tenor voice
¿De un joto?

¿Cómo?

Porque mis gritos son norteños
De un macho y de mi padre
Y no de Lucha o la Lola
Because I contest and defy
Your estereotipos
Y falsas ilusiones

JESÚS ALONZO

Y no ando con vestido
O peluca
Ni con lipstick
O la mano caída
And because I am not effeminate
I cannot be a joto?

Pues, how tragic!

¡Me lleva la chingada!
¡Porque un joto
Mero mero joto
Jotinchón
Es exactamente lo que soy yo!

(He lets out a grito. The music comes back. He resumes dancing.)

(BLACKOUT)

(END OF SCENE)

Scene 7

Straight on Queers Infomercial:
Video Installment #2

(The video opens to the previous scene of the HOST in the television studio. Prerecorded applause is heard.)

HOST

(Excitedly.) What joto doesn't want to have the know-how to shut ignorance up? Now you can! For only $19.95, plus shipping and handling, *Straight on Queers*, will be delivered right to your front door. And if within the first two viewings of this video you do not see changes in how you respond to homophobia, you can return it for a full refund. Yes, you heard correctly! We stand by *Straight on Queers* so confidently that we guarantee your complete satisfaction or your money back! But your money is the last thing you'll want after watching *Straight on Queers*.

(Seriously now.) We at Jotas Concientizadas, Inc. consulted with the world's leading joto experts and quick-mouthed divas to put this video together. We carefully studied the ignorance about us that permeates society. The result is this four hour video, guaranteed to turn you into a fast-tongued, quick thinking, all-knowing jota concientizada! But you don't have to take my word for it!

(The scene cuts to a professor's office where the intellectual DR. TOMÁS P. NE prestigiously sits behind his desk. Captions revealing his name and title appear: Dr. Tomás P. Ne, Ph.D., Jota Studies Expert.)

DR. TOMÁS P. NE

I am Tomás P. Ne, Doctor of Jotería. In all my years of study I never saw such wonderful work of conscientization put together for our gente jota. Having worked closely with Jotas Concientizadas, Inc., I too became a stronger willed, quick-minded, sharp-tongued queena. I highly recommend this work that is comprised of pure joto sabiduría.

(The camera zooms to a close-up of DR. TOMÁS P. NE, who suddenly grins proudly.)

Well, I'm not just a spokesperson; I'm also a very satisfied customer!

(VIDEO OUT)

(END OF SCENE)

Scene 8

Night Madness Poem

(A solitary man appears on stage and speaks directly to the audience.)

Do you recognize
me
unmasked
and free of all the binding skins
construed
by this world?

Tell me,
amá, apá
do you know who
I am:
your secretive son
who lives in a world
he
holds between two fingers
unveiled
molding and remolding
shaping and reshaping
eternally frustrated
emotionally deficient
loving you so truthfully
truth fails him
for your own protection?

Do you know
who he is:
your child who awakens
before the aurora
free of guilt
in damp sheets

JESÚS ALONZO

with a full, throbbing erection
and cold sweat rushes
yelling out the names of men
— ¡Che! ¡Emiliano! ¡Marcos!
¡Augusto! ¡Paolo! ¡Jesús! ¡José!
¡Zumbi! —
like when he was a child
fearing the monster in his closet?

And how 'bout you,
hermanas,
can you speak of who
I am?
Your bold young brother,
fearless of public opinion
outlandish in dress code
the revolutionary soul soldier
wearing a French beret
his big black boots
and grandma's silk scarf around his neck
Do you recognize
me:
your little brother
ready to alter the state of nature
and the nature of the state
who dreams of writing books
and speaks of Liberation Theologies
Socialism, Communism, Anarchism
race, sex
and concientización?

And my brothers,
do you recognize
me:
the sissy on the
sidelines of our annual
Thanksgiving street football game
the one who prefers to
run alone
than to play on any man's team
mamma's boy
who cannot fight
but will surely tell
anyone about their
bad looks, bad breath
poor reasoning skills
and barbaric ways?
Yes,
the child who kicked
your ass with words
while you kicked his
with your fists and knees
and still said,
"It don't hurt!"
Do you recognize
me
with no known mate
nor plans of womanizing
or courting a lady?

¿Y mi pueblo
qué dice?
Do you know of me
and others like me

JESÚS ALONZO

who breathe
only
the air at night
while you sleep
and who live
only
among your shadows and memories?

Do you know of the masks we wear
around you
around everyone?
Do you know
who we are,
what we are,
what we do?
Can you recognize
us?
Do you recognize
me:
This faggot,
this outcast,
this phenomenon in nature?
What can you say
you know about
this jotinchón?

(BLACKOUT)

(END OF SCENE)

Scene 9

El Pinche Rapist

(At rise, there is a small dimly lit living room. There is an old television set, middle stage right, sitting in front of a worn sofa, center stage. Extra light is provided in the background by a lamp that sits on a small coffee table to the right of the sofa. There is also a small dresser, back stage left that serves as a makeshift altar. It is adorned with several candles, saints' statues, mementos, and a single 8x10 black and white photo of FATHER'S late wife. FATHER sits on the couch, preparing to watch a boxing match. After a short pause, his 16-year-old son PEDRO walks in the room from front stage left. He carries himself awkwardly around FATHER and always maintains a physical distance.)

FATHER

Hey, mi'jo, you got here just in time. The fight is about to start. Come sit with me.

PEDRO

¿Cómo está, apá?

FATHER

Pues ya me vez mi'jo, aquí nomás, getting older and uglier.

PEDRO

(Smiling.) Don't say that. You look fine.

FATHER

(Noticing.) What's wrong, mi'jo? ¿Estás bien?

PEDRO

No, nada.

(Short pause.) Apá, can we talk?

(A bell rings off stage signifying the beginning of the fight.)

FATHER

Can we talk later, mi'jo? The fight's just getting started.

(Pauses to watch the television then back to PEDRO.) Ándale, sit down and watch it with me.

PEDRO

No, apá, I think I'll just come back later.

(PEDRO begins to walk off front stage left.)

FATHER

¡Mi'jo!

(PEDRO stops to look back.) ¿Qué te pasa?

PEDRO

Nothing, dad. En serio. There's nothing wrong.

FATHER

(Going up to PEDRO.) Órale, mi'jo, don't be lying to your old man now!

PEDRO

I'm not lying to you, dad. I'm fine.

FATHER

(Looking into PEDRO'S face.) Then what happened to your eyes? They look red. You been crying?

PEDRO

No, apá, nothing's wrong.

(PEDRO crosses to center stage, away from FATHER.) I was just thinking, you know...

FATHER

(Acknowledging the make-shift altar.) About your mamá, ¿pues no?

PEDRO

About everything, apá.

(Short pause. PEDRO crosses behind couch as FATHER attempts
to come up to him center stage.) But it's okay, we'll talk later. Después
hablamos.

FATHER

(Taken aback by the distance.) Órale, mi'jo, stop acting like a chick!

(Sits again.) Come sit here.

(FATHER pauses shortly to watch the television. A bell rings off stage to
signify the end of round one.)

Look, there's a commercial. Let's talk.

(PEDRO crosses back and takes a seat at the opposite end of FATHER.)

What's wrong, mi'jo? Why do you feel so sad?

PEDRO

I'm not sad. I was just thinking that something might not be right with me.

FATHER

What do you mean, mi'jo? Are you sick?

(Crosses to PEDRO and feels his forehead with his hand.) No vayas a
andar resfriado.

PEDRO

(Pushing FATHER back.) No, apá, I'm not sick. My temperature's fine.

(FATHER takes his seat again.) The thing is that...

(Short pause.) I don't even know where to start. Sometimes I feel a little
weird inside. Así, algo extraño.

PEDRO (Continued.)

(As PEDRO speaks, we hear a bell ring off stage to signify the beginning of round two. FATHER begins to watch television again and no longer pays attention to PEDRO.)

I love women, don't get me wrong; my mother was a woman. But, apá, that's the only way I think I could ever love a woman, like a mother or maybe even a sister, or a friend. What do you think, apá? Hey, apá? ¿Qué piensa?

FATHER
(Still watching television.) What do I think about what, mi'jo?

PEDRO
About what I just told you.

FATHER
(Turns to PEDRO.) Pues what did you just tell me?

PEDRO
¡Apá! You ask me to tell you what's bothering me and when I tell you, you ignore me! I gotta go. We'll talk later.

(Gets up to leave.)

FATHER
(Reaches toward PEDRO but still watches the television.) Mi'jo, ¡espérate, hombre!

(Short pause.) Just let the second round finish.

(To television as PEDRO stands by.) ¡Eso! ¡Dale en la madre a ese maricón! ¡Show 'em what a real man is made of! ¡Puto!

(A bell rings off stage signifying the end of round two.)

FATHER (Continued.)

¡Híjole! ¡Le van a dar en la mera madre! That round was rough!

(To PEDRO.) Ahora sí, mi'jo. Dime, ¿qué te pasa? What's bothering you?

PEDRO

Apá, it's not easy to tell you what I have to say.

(Retakes his seat at the opposite end of FATHER.) I was telling you that I love women, but I don't think it's exactly like a man should...

FATHER

(Confused.) ¿Qué me estás diciendo, mi'jo?

PEDRO

Nothing. It's just I am not sure if there is something wrong with me. What if...

FATHER

(Interrupting.) Of course there's nothing wrong with you, mi'jo! You're only sixteen years old. ¡Estás bien huerco! Don't worry because you don't have a girlfriend yet. Some day a good vieja will come your way. You just wait and see.

PEDRO

But, apá, I don't think that's ever gonna happen.

FATHER

(Taken aback.) And why not, mi'jo?

PEDRO

(Gets up and crosses behind the sofa.) Well, apá, because I think that I don't like women.

FATHER

Ay, mi'jo, how are you not going to like viejas? You have to! ¡Eres hombre!

JESÚS ALONZO

PEDRO

(Carefully.) Well, apá, I don't; and I don't think it's ever gonna happen.

(A bell rings off stage signifying the beginning of round three.)

FATHER

¡Órale, mi'jo! Then what?

(Laughing.) ¿Te gustan los pinches viejos?

PEDRO

(Nervously.) Apá, I'm not even sure that I know if...

FATHER

(Interrupting and searching for an explanation.) Pues of course, mi'jo. Of course you're gonna like men. They're the only true friends in life. Las viejas, ¡ni pa' que trostiarlas! Chicks are always running their mouth and making you feel bad about yourself!

PEDRO

But apá, I think that I could love a man as more than just a friend or a father even. It's a weird feeling. I don't know if it's wrong or not. I don't know what to do.

FATHER

(Standing up.) ¿Qué...qué...qué chingados? What are you telling me, son, that you're a fucking joto, ¿o qué fregados?

PEDRO

Don't say it like that, apá. It's like I told you. I-I-I don't know.

FATHER

(Outraged.) Joto, maricón, faggot, queer, say it how you want, it's all the same shit anyway.

PEDRO

Apá, I'm telling you that I...

FATHER

(Interrupting.) You're fucked up, son! I taught you to be a man, mi'jo, and that's exactly what you need to be. ¡No vengas a decirme esas tonterías!

PEDRO

Pero, apá, what if, what if I am a ho-homo-homosexual?

FATHER

(Shouting.) How do you know, man?

PEDRO

I'm telling you I don't! But I think I might be.

(A bell rings off stage signifying the end of round three.)

FATHER

(FATHER comes behind sofa, opposite PEDRO.) Pedro Manuel, you shut your mouth right now!

PEDRO

Please try to understand. These are my feelings. I-I-I need to get them out. They're eating me up inside, apá! I can't be quiet anymore. I feel weird.. I need to talk to…to…

(Short pause.) You're my best friend. You're my only friend.

FATHER

(Charges toward PEDRO and grabs him.) ¡Pedro Manuel Cervantes!

PEDRO

(Trying to get away.) ¡Apá!

FATHER

There's nothing to talk about. You're fucked up, mi'jo!

(Releases PEDRO.) I didn't bring you up so that you could fuck faggots. ¿Qué te pasa?

PEDRO

(Uncertain.) What's wrong with me? Nothing's wrong with me. I don't know. I need to talk with someone...with someone I love, someone I trust.

FATHER

¡Que te callaras el hocico, perro! Ya te dije, there is nothing to talk about!

PEDRO

No, apá, no me callo. ¡No puedo! This is how I feel. And if I am...if I am a homosexual, then I need you to know. But I am not sure. I need to know it for myself first.

(A bell rings off stage signifying the beginning of round four.)

FATHER

(Charges PEDRO again.) So you want to fuck men, pendejo? Eh? Tell me!

PEDRO

(Pulling back, terrified.) No, it's not like that, apá!

FATHER

(Slaps PEDRO across the face.) Ah, so then you want them to fuck you!

PEDRO

No, apá, don't say it like that...

FATHER

Then how should I say it? Think about the shit you're saying!

PEDRO

Apá, I know what I'm saying! It's...it's how I feel.

FATHER

(Slaps PEDRO who falls to the floor behind the sofa.) So you do want to get fucked by faggots!

(FATHER comes behind the sofa and stands above PEDRO.)

PEDRO

(Attempting to get up and away from FATHER.)

¡No, apá! Stop hitting me! You're hurting me!

FATHER

(Looking down on PEDRO.) Pues que bueno because that's exactly what they're gonna do to you!

(FATHER charges at PEDRO as PEDRO attempts to get up from the floor.)

Why can't you see how things really are, pendejo?

(PEDRO and FATHER fall to the ground and we hear them struggle with one another behind the sofa.)

PEDRO

¡No, apá! Please stop it! Please, I'm...I'm...

FATHER

You're what? Scared? ¿Pues no que you could love a man as more than just a friend or a father?

(FATHER pins PEDRO to the ground.)

¡Órale pues! Here's a real fucking man for you, then!

(FATHER begins to rip PEDRO'S clothes and undo his own belt and pants.)

PEDRO

(More terrified than before.) Apá, what are you doing?

(As they struggle on the ground, FATHER begins to sexually force himself on PEDRO and rapes him.)

PEDRO (Continued.)

Stop! ¡Para! ¿Qué estas haciendo, apá? What are you doing?

(There is a short pause as the struggle ensues.)

You're hurting me!

FATHER

This is what they do with each other, cabrón! ¡Pinches maricones! That's all they know how to do.

PEDRO

Stop, I told you! Please! ¡Por el amor de Dios! Please stop! ¡Por el amor de mi madre! Stop!

FATHER

Don't even mention your mother, pendejo, because if she were alive she'd be ashamed of you! ¿Me oyes? ¡Te tuviera vergüenza!

(FATHER spits on PEDRO'S face.)

PEDRO

(Desperate.) ¡Para, apá! ¡Ya te dije, para!

(A bell rings off stage signifying the end of round four. PEDRO manages to finally set himself free from FATHER and runs off front stage left into the audience.)

FATHER

Get back here pendejo!

(FATHER freezes.)

PEDRO

(PEDRO wheezes and tries to collect himself. He speaks to the audience.)

Why did he have to do this to me?

PEDRO (Continued.)

(Short pause.) First he tore my pants open and then he ripped off my underwear.

(Struggling.) And he held me there, like an animal, like I wasn't even his blood. And then he...he forced it in me.

(Sobbing.) And I was yelling because it hurt! Fuck, it hurt! He knew it too. But he didn't stop. He didn't stop. When I was able to get away, I just ran out of the house. I just ran and ran. I shut my eyes but I could still see him above me. And I could hear his voice in my head, "¡Pendejo! ¡Pendejo! ¡Pendejo!" He's never called me that before!

(Sobs and then yells.) No, no, no! I'm not a pendejo! I am not a pendejo!

(PEDRO begins to exit the theater house.)

¡Ay, Dios! ¡Ay, Dios mío!

(PEDRO stops and looks back to FATHER who is still frozen on stage.)

How could you? You're all I have! How could you? I'm your only son! How could you? How?

(PEDRO exits theater house, defeated.)

FATHER

(Unfreezes.) How could I what? Teach you the truth about things, how they really are? ¡Pendejo! One day you'll see that your father was right. Algún día verás.

(FATHER suddenly turns to the picture of his late wife and begins to walk toward makeshift altar.)

¿Qué fregados? Don't look at me that way, Tina! What I did is not wrong.

FATHER (Continued.)

What I did is not wrong! You hear me? He'll see one day and he'll thank me for it. You just wait, you just wait, I tell you.

(FATHER takes the picture in his hands and continues to speak to it as he crosses to center stage in front of sofa.)

I love Pedro. I didn't bring him up to be a maricón. What the fuck is wrong with him? Since the day you passed away and left us ,Tina, I've wanted only the best for our Pedro. He's our only son y mi único amigo.

(Short pause.) ¡Chingado!

(FATHER places picture down on the coffee table.)

He's all I got left in this world. I bust my ass for him! Why does he have to tell me these stupid things? ¿Qué le pasa a ese muchacho? What's wrong with him?

(FATHER sits on the sofa in front of the television.)

TELEVISION ANNOUNCER
(Off stage.) ...and your new heavyweight champion is...

FATHER
(FATHER turns off the television with the remote control.)

¡Ya ni la pinche pelea vi!

(BLACKOUT)

(END OF SCENE)

Act II

Scene 1

Straight on Queers Infomercial:
Video Installment #3

(The video opens to a scene of two men talking at the restroom urinals while making use of the facilities.)

VOICEOVER
Are you tired of ignorant statements about our joto lifestyle?

(VOICEOVER out as the volume comes up on the men's conversation.)

STRAIGHT MAN
What I am saying is that I just don't understand this gay shit. I mean, who's on top anyway?

(Video freezes.)

VOICEOVER
Then put a dead stop to these slanders and spread some joto sabiduría with *Straight on Queers!*

(Video resumes.)

JOTO
¡No, Cheto! The issue here is not that you do not understand. What you are really saying is that you do not know.

(Inquisitively.) Allow me to ask, do you and your wife still have sex?

STRAIGHT MAN
Hell yeah!

JOTO
And who's on top there?

STRAIGHT MAN

Well she is!

(Catches himself.) I mean, I am! I mean, it depends on whatever mood we're in.

JOTO

All right then. It works the same way for jotos. Sometimes a guy may want to be on top, other times he may want to be on the bottom. It all depends on whatever mood we're in.

(Suddenly inquisitive again.) Would you ever take it up the rear?

STRAIGHT MAN

(Offended, a bleep covers his curse word.) @U*K no! That's not what I'm about!

JOTO

The same goes for jotos! Some of us would never take it up the rear, others take it exclusively up the rear, and yet others are so highly versatile that they take it any which way it comes: top or bottom, left or right, bocarriba or bocabajo. And why is that? Because when it comes to sex, that is either what we are or are not about! Punto final. What is there left to understand, my friend?

STRAIGHT MAN

(Shyly inquisitive.) Uh, is it gay that I like my ass played with?

(VIDEO OUT)

(END OF SCENE)

JESÚS ALONZO

Scene 2

Janie la Transie

(At rise, we see a bedroom with women's clothes, fashion magazines, and school textbooks strewn about. JANIE sits at her dresser applying make-up and getting dressed for work. "American Woman" by Tommy and the Who, plays in the background. JANIE suddenly acknowledges the audience, lowers the volume on her radio and speaks.)

JANIE

That I'm a freak of nature. That's what they used to tell me. That I would never make it in the real world, sólo porque soy lo que soy. That's what they used to say. But if they only knew then what I know now. Pues look at me: a sophisticated, successful career woman and part-time student. Oh, did I say woman? Well good because that's exactly what I am, a beautifully created woman. Capital W-O-M-A-N. I am my own creation; my very own work of art. Style is my sustenance, glamour my biological make-up.

(Changes tone.) But I wasn't always like this. My birth name is Juan Navarro, but that's what they called me when I was still my mommy's hombrecito.

(Laughing.) Whatever that means. After I became the goddess that you see before you, I took the name Janie. Don't get me wrong. Don't think that I wanted to pass for a gabacha, it's only that the name Juana didn't have a nice ring to it. I mean, not to offend any Juana's out there, but you have to admit that it does have a pretty ugly ring to it.

(Disgustedly emphasizes each syllable.) Jua-na. ¡Ay no, qué feo! And besides, that was the name of my 'buelita's pig in México. I didn't want to have a marrana's name! Would you? Y además, it even rhymes con marrana. Can you imagine? People would look at me and say, "Eh, ¡allí va Juana la marrana!"

(Laughing.) Anyways. Before, la gente me decía que no one would ever take me seriously because I wasn't a real woman; that I wouldn't make it.

They thought I was some eccentric, sideshow circus freak. But I proved them wrong, every last one of them. Yo soy bien ambitious y sé luchar. I'm the type of girl who goes out for what she wants. And I always get it. I have so far. Check this. During the day, I work at the mall.

(Nodding her head approvingly.) Yes, I have a job! Pues qué pensaban, that I'm some useless, lazy queen? Or perhaps you had already stereotyped me, huh? Did you think I was one of those female impersonators at the gay clubs?

(Aside.) Not that there's anything wrong with that. But I could never match up to those girls. I can't lip sync to save my life! Y deja tú, I cringe at the sight of duct tape! Oh no, honey! My thing is fashion and clothes, particularly calzones. I love me a good pair of panties! Sabes, I'm a manager for the Victoria's Secrets. You should come by some time; we have great sales. I just love it when the silk thongs go on sale. Um, that's when I stock up, girl. And it's a really good deal! You buy two pairs and you get the third one free. Try and beat that! Oh, but let me tell you, we also have those matte satin boxer pajamas. The real sexy ones. There's nothing I like better after a long hard day than coming home and relaxing in my black satin boxer pajamas. They're so butch-a-la-femme! Oh, but we also have very, very nice bras. My personal favorite is of course, the Miracle Bra! It makes your chichis stand up nice and erect, like two little soldiers ready for battle. And the extra padding, well it just gives those of us less fortunate girls a bit more to show for, if you know what I mean. And for a bra with wires, it's excellent! No te cala like the other bras they sell at the Sears or Wal-Mart.

(Suddenly catches herself.) Ay, but look at me, already trying to make a sale off you guys. I just love being around chones all day. But lately I've been thinking about quitting my job, pero no sé. I'm not too sure. The thing is that it's tiring for me because I also go to school. Oh, that's right! I didn't tell you. Pues I'm studying Business Administration, girl! I'm about to finish my B.A. Can you believe it? But I'm not stopping there. In two more years I'll have my M.B.A. también. You see my real dream is to have my very own lingerie boutique. I want to be my own boss. I realized this one day when this vieja at the store got angry because I wasn't a real woman. As if! So she complained to my boss. She said it was wrong and immoral for people like

JESÚS ALONZO

me to be serving the public. But my boss is very open-minded and she has her wits in the right place. She knows a good worker when she sees one. And besides, she already knew about me when she hired me. But you know how it goes in retail, "the customer is always right!" So my boss asked me to stay in the stock room when closed-minded viejas came into the store. At first I did, but the more I thought about it, the less sense it all made. Closed-minded viejas at Victoria's Secrets? For God's sake, we sell thongs and lingerie, among other risqué foundation! I hope our customers come in with an open mind. And besides, I think that if some pinche vieja has a problem with me, then that's exactly what it is: it's her problem, not mine. I'm perfectly happy with who I am. Y además, I have a job to do, and that job, to be precise, is to serve the public, regardless of what I may personally think of any of them. Then one day while I was in the stock room taking inventory, I started thinking that it would be nice to have my very own lingerie boutique. Just the thought of selecting what panties to put up for sale drives me wild. But more than that, I want to have my very own lingerie boutique because I want viejas like the one I mentioned to come into my shop and get angry when they find out that I am not what they consider a real woman. And when they get ready to complain, I want them to ask for my boss so that I can say, "I am the boss, honey, and if you have a problem with me, then I have no business with you and you have no business putting your filthy hands on my chones! ¡Poochie, pá fuera de mi shop!" Mmm, mmm! ¡Ya estoy cansada de quedarme callada! I will be quiet no longer! That's why I decided to go back to school. I thought, maybe I should get an education; it can't hurt me because it will only help me realize my dream. Y además, I'd be learning lots of stuff. I've always said learning is good. Pero también, I decided to go back to school because I don't want to be like the dumb vieja who came into the store and insulted me. I want to be exposed to new people and ideas. They do say that education opens your mind; and I agree. I mean, who wants to be una ignorante who lives within the confines of a tiny, gated microcosm anyway? Talk about a false sense of security! Not me, honey. ¡No, señor! My gates are open to the world! I want to be as intelligent a person as possible. So I hit the books hard and try to stay real focused because this is what I want, and I know that this is what I'll get. And why? Porque como ya les dije, soy bien ambitious y sé luchar.

(Short pause.) Hmm, now that I think about it, I shouldn't quit my job. Pues how am I going to pay for my education? And if I can't get my education, how will I ever get the know-how to properly administer the financial matters of my shop? I'll just have to stick it out for now –ignorant people and all – right? Pero I'm a firm believer que ¡sí se puede!

(Proudly.) ¡Yo sé luchar! I know it's possible, no matter what people tell me. Yo no soy una ignorante. I'll keep making it in life. This is one success story that has yet to be written. My dreams will come true!

(American Woman begins to play anew. JANIE dances as she finishes getting dressed.)

(BLACKOUT)

(END OF SCENE)

JESÚS ALONZO

Scene 3

Jotería

(At rise, PONCHO and FELIPE sit at a busy street corner, conversing and watching passersby.)

FELIPE

Hey, Poncho, heard any good joto jokes lately?

PONCHO

(Annoyed). Nah, Felipe, not really.

FELIPE

Pues aquí te va uno...

PONCHO

Alright, vato, but keep it clean.

FELIPE

Ay, pues what are you? Suddenly te crees la Mother Teresa o qué, dude? You know joto jokes ain't clean. They gotta be dirty like the maricones!

PONCHO

(Irritated.) ¡Ya, vato! Forget it. Just tell the damn joke already.

FELIPE

Okay, Poncho, this one's just for you.

(Standing up.) There's these two jotos, right, and they're talking about what they had did the night before and the first maricón says,

(Mocks each characters' voice effeminately.) "Hey girl, pues where were you last night? I looked all over the place for you." And the second one responds, "No pues I was over at Miguel's and guess what? We made mole!" "Mole? Get outta here," says the first joto. "I didn't know you knew how to make mole." "Well it's real simple," tells him the second joto. "Pues I

FELIPE (Continued.)

wouldn't even know where to start or even know what to put in the mole, girl!" So the second joto starts to explain, así, like a real fucking mole expert, "It's real simple. Mira, all you put in it is the toast bread, el chocolate, el ajonjolí, la peanut butter, chile pasilla, chile cascabel, chile mulato, chile ancho, chile…" And then all of a sudden the first joto screams, "¡Ay! ¡Ya para, girl! Don't tell me no more! All this talk of chile is making my ass water!"

(FELIPE lets out a loud laugh.)

PONCHO

(Indifferent.) That's sick, Felipe! Why you gotta go there?

FELIPE

Ay. Poncho, chill-out! Mira, here goes another one.

PONCHO

(Aside.) Oh, great!

FELIPE

There's two compadres about to take their lunch break at work. One's a tall big guy and the other one is a güero, kinda like me. They're walking out to the taco truck when the tall one says,

(In a deep, rough voice.) "Óigame, pinche compadre, they told me you're going around telling people that we were kissing!" And the güero, así, todo alarmed tells 'em,

(Worried.) "¡Ni pensar, compadre! How can you even imagine that I'd go around saying such a thing?" And then the tall one says,

(Suddenly effeminately.) "Ay, pues, compadre, then I guess they must've seen us!"

(FELIPE lets out another loud laugh as PONCHO looks on annoyed.)

¡Pinches jotos, todos son iguálales!

PONCHO

Oh yeah, Felipe? How do you figure that?

FELIPE

They're all the same shit man, no matter how you look at it!

(Pantomiming.) Mira, se portan como las viejas, andan como las viejas, hablan como las viejas...

(Suddenly to PONCHO, as a matter-of-factly.) ...and they're all sluts!

PONCHO

(Standing.) And I bet all they do is have sex with each other all day long, ¿qué no?

FELIPE

That's why they call them homo-sexo-uales!

PONCHO

¿En serio, Felipe? ¡No! Get outta here!

FELIPE

Pues what'd you think, Poncho?

PONCHO

Pues no, Felipe, I guess you're right because they do call normal people homo sapiens...

FELIPE

(Interrupting.) Didn't I tell you? Now you're thinking, vato!

PONCHO

(Humoring FELIPE.) But wait a minute Felipe. They also call normal people heterosexuals. A ver, how do you figure that one?

FELIPE

Ay, Poncho, pues where'd you go to school, man? They didn't teach you right! You are the child left behind, dude!

(Explaining.) Mira, normal people can be called homo sapiens or heterosexuals because we either have sex or we don't. We have sex sometimes, but not all the time...

PONCHO

Like the homo-sexo-uales!

FELIPE

¡Exactamente!

(Short pause.) And if you pay attention to the last part of the word, you'll see that it even rhymes with iguales!

PONCHO

(Suddenly confused.) ¿Y esa?

FELIPE

Ay, Poncho, ¡pues porque los homo-sexo-uales son todos iguales!

PONCHO

You're right, vato. It all makes sense to me now. ¡Todos los jotos sí son iguales!

(Imitating FELIPE.) They're all sexo-maniacos!

FELIPE

They're all the same caca, vato! And have you ever noticed que andan todos con la mano caída?

(FELIPE mimics hand gestures.)

PONCHO

Pero wait a minute Felipe, tu dad también anda con la mano caída.

JESÚS ALONZO

FELIPE

(Suddenly infuriated.) ¡Cállate el hocico, buey! That's a war wound! Man, vato, how can you even say that? Psss....baboso....the insinuation alone, vato...

PONCHO

(Defusing FELIPE.) Okay, okay, perdón. I didn't know your dad was a veterano.

FELIPE

Yeah, man! He was in the Bexar County Correctional.

PONCHO

(To audience.) Is that a war?

FELIPE

(No longer angry.) Hey, Poncho, have you ever thought why they call jotos gay?

PONCHO

That's easy, vato! They call jotos gay because they're always happy.

FELIPE

(Sitting down.) That's what I thought! So why do they also call them jotos?

PONCHO

¡Ay, Felipe! Because it's like you said, man, they're sluts —hoe-tos? They're hoes!

FELIPE

Goddamn! I didn't know that.

PONCHO

(Coming up to FELIPE.) Well now you do. Hey vato, I gotta go. Ay te watcho, camacho...

FELIPE

No-no-no-no-no-no-no, wait a minute. I'm not done yet. I got another question for you. A ver, why do they call jotos fags?

PONCHO

(Thinking.) Pues the word fag means a lot of things, Felipe. But in Britain, cigarettes are called fags.

FELIPE

(Confused.) So what's that gotta do with jotos? Are you telling me they're British? Con razón hablan tan funny!

PONCHO

No, Felipe. Think about it. What do you do to get the smoke out of a cigarette?

FELIPE

Pues you...

(Suddenly realizing.) ...you suck on it!

PONCHO

It works the same way for jotos. In order to get your dick fix...

FELIPE

(Interrupting.) ...you gotta suck on the fag! ¡En la madre, Poncho! Estás bien smart, vato!

PONCHO

(Bashfully.) Well I wouldn't go that far, Felipe? I was just fu...

FELIPE

(Suddenly interrupting, suspiciously.) Hey, wait a minute. How's it that all of a sudden you know so much about jotos? Just a little while ago Mother Teresa here didn't know why they even call jotos homo-sexo-uales.

PONCHO

¡Ay, Felipe! Dude, I gotta go.

FELIPE

(Stands up and walks toward PONCHO.)

No, really, Poncho. Now you tell me.

PONCHO

(Hesitating.) Okay, vato.

(Then suddenly confident.) Sabes qué, I gotta joke for you now.

(Motions for FELIPE to sit next to him.) There's these two vatos, right, one just like me and the other one, pues, just like you. One day they're sittin' out on the street, you know, just shootin' the shit and making fun of jotos.

FELIPE

(Excited.) Oh, man, this joke is good already!

PONCHO

So the first vato, the one who's just like you, ends up telling these really fucked up, dumb-ass jokes about jotos that only he laughs at. But the second vato, the one who's just like me, he doesn't laugh, because, not only are the jokes not funny, but he's also a joto and that shit is really offensive to him. You get it?

(FELIPE laughs uncontrollably then stops suddenly.)

FELIPE

(Confused.) Wait a minute, vato. I don't get it?

PONCHO

(Standing up.) Felipe, you asked how come I know so much about jotos. Pues for the reals, I just fed you the same bullshit you served me. I don't know much, but I do know this: I am a joto, and since we are all the same

PONCHO (Continued.)

I thought you'd be able to figure it out. But I guess I was wrong. ¡Allí te watcho!

(Begins to coolly walk off stage then stops to look at FELIPE.)

Vato, you're so queer!

FELIPE

Wh-what the fu...

(BLACKOUT)

(END OF SCENE)

In the Shadow of Gayness

(A lone man recites the poem.)

"Pero tú no pareces joto,"
tells me a hetero colleague
whom until now I've admired
for being so damn queer friendly.

Tells me I don't look gay
and thinks I'll be
complimented,
expects, perhaps,
a sigh of relief to come
out from deep within my soul.

But instead I'm appalled
and even walled
by this level of ignorance
because
I've seen too much,
been too many places
fought too many battles
to accept this catch-22
pervasively homophobic
complimenting insult
[slash]
insulting compliment.
And
I'm tired of
being on the defensive,
setting off the offensive.

Therefore,
this being an issue that
concerns and even consumes many of my kind –
preoccupies us even
that we not
look like what we are
ignoring the fact that we are what we look like –
today I approach the problem with a different tactic
and instead I respond with a question.

Tell me, my unknowingly
homophobic friend,
what does gay look like?
Because I've seen this image
portrayed in doctors and teachers
athletes and artists
men of the clergy and drug fiends
drag queens and drag racers;
I've seen it
portrayed on battle fields by soldiers
and by mothers and fathers of natural born
and adopted children;
this image suffers on the streets
dies in cold, lonely desolate hospital wards
shops at the mall
and harvests acres and acres of agricultural plots;
it
sits behind the desks of CEOs and law firms
plays leading roles in movies
and labors at construction sites.

This gay image I've seen
almost everywhere
in everyone
and in everything.
Yet you tell me,
a citizen of this world,
that I do not look gay?

JESÚS ALONZO

Who's world do you
live in
anyway?
Because if you'd
stop to take a look around
you'd see
that I in fact look very gay.
I tell you
that if you'd stop and look a little more,
look a little closer,
you'd see
that you,
who is also a citizen of this world,
look mighty gay too.

(BLACK OUT)

(END OF SCENE)

Scene 5

Vicente

(REMINISCENT JOTO, a casually dressed man wearing jeans and a button-down shirt, crosses from back stage right to stage center. He speaks to the audience as he crosses the stage. Semi-distorted images of city buses, bus stops, and people on the streets project behind him.)

REMINISCENT JOTO

His memory still haunts me
The steady glance
His deep, dark-eyed gaze
Burning still
Into the totality of my core

I first saw him
Amidst my working class gente
Hotel workers and
Restaurant waiters
Nurses
Day laborers
I vaguely remember
Some vagrants
A couple of students
Several drunks
The foolish man
Whom with me, made two
But none of them matter
They are all blurred
But he remains
Fresh
Crisp
Clear
Deeply impressed
Into the memory of my soul

Feathered orange dyed hair
A blond treatment that didn't take
Perfectly manicured eyebrows
À la Chola-Gretta Garbo-style
His thick-chain rope necklace
The dangling gold medallion
Bearing the image of the Guadalupana
His delicate hands
As fragile
As his frame appeared
Clasping a black windbreaker
That contrasted
His lengthy polished nails
The crisp white uniform
The brass plated nametag bearing his name:
Vicente
I remember it weighing heavily
On the left side of his chest
Heavy like this single memory
That causes such great unrest

That evening
As I boarded the city bus
I saw him
And saw what I was escaping
It wasn't my home
Nor was it my city
No era mi familia
Ni tampoco mi gente
It was me
The true me
That I desperately concealed
Within the shell of the un-me

With his simple look
The hope behind his eyes
The sudden rush of blood

I am certain we both felt
He noticed me
Recognized me
Instantly knew who I was
But not from an old friendship
Nor anytime before
It was joto-intuition
A powerful beyond cosmic force
That revealed the undeniable secret
Plotting my life course

Taking my seat
The foolish man I sat next to
Turned to me and shouted

(A male silhouette emerges from back stage right.)

FOOLISH MAN

¡Hey, holmes!
¡Wátchate el marica,

REMINISCENT JOTO

Motioning his head
Toward Vicente,

FOOLISH MAN

¡Ese pinche jotinchón!
Parece vieja la puta,
Hey bro,
¡Se ve que le gusta
La verga al cabrón!

REMINISCENT JOTO

I heard other men laughing
Retching their cruel, hateful, menacing delight
But I sat there in silence
Frozen by fear even greater

JESÚS ALONZO

Than the greatest pain
I could dare to bare

FOOLISH MAN

No me digas que te gusta,

REMINISCENT JOTO

Continued the fool
Half-joking
Half-probing

FOOLISH MAN

¿A poco también eres maricón?

(Silhouette disappears.)

REMINISCENT JOTO

Madly, I looked over
Beginning to speak
I sprung forward
"No seas pendejo,
Baboso"
I told him
Instantly deciding
My truth
Was too dangerous
And I was too weak

"Cómo crees que soy marica"
I continued
Turning to
Vicente
Staring him down
As I spoke
"Do I look like that faggot?
¡Pinche joto!
Sí es cierto,

REMINISCENT JOTO (Continued.)

¡Parece vieja la puta
Ese pinche jotinchón!"

Then the fool started laughing
The other men laughed harder than before
I remained stoic
But deep inside
I was crying
For what I said to Vicente
For being a coward
For finding comfort in knowing
That within their hate I was safe

Still looking,
I noticed Vicente
Begin to sit up
He cleared his throat
And I swallowed hard
I became more terrified than before
He knew my truth
It was now his turn
To roast me
Serve me
Deliver my ashes
Tell these men my sorry-ass self-worth

Instead
He glanced at me sympathetically
The men in the background still laughing
Vicente cracked a hard smile
And took a deep breath
Disapprovingly nodding his head
Then he looked away
Ashamed of my shame
And my self-hating words
I just sat there

JESÚS ALONZO

Choking on my lie
Drowning in his gaze
The rest of the ride home
Wishing I could rise to the level of his courage
Destroy all the hate around us
Lovingly embrace him
Beg my joto-brother's forgiveness

(BLACKOUT)

(END OF SCENE)

Scene 6

¡Carnal!

(At rise, CARNAL stands at a bus stop listening to a conversation between the CHOLO and two other guys.)

CHOLO
(Speaking loudly and laughing.) Nah man, I fuckin' can't stand faggots. Vato, I swear if I ever saw one, I'll kick his ass. Make 'em feel real sorry he was ever born.

(CARNAL becomes nervous and lights a cigarette. This gets the CHOLO'S attention.)

Hey, ¡carnal! Hey, ¡carnal!

CARNAL
Hey, ¡carnal!
you call onto me
when just seconds ago you
told your homies how much
you hate faggots. That
God forbid you ever ran into
one, for his sake, because
you'd kick his faggot ass —break
every faggot limb of
his faggot body.

CHOLO
Hey, ¡carnal!

CARNAL
you call onto me. And I
remain indifferent,
unresponsive.

JESÚS ALONZO

I suck on my cigarette. Hide
behind its smoke
for fear of being identified;
I
look down the street
opposite your direction
hoping to see the bus
that just won't come.

CHOLO

Hey, ¡carnal!

CARNAL

And your homies begin to step
in my direction. Other people
waiting for the bus
look over our way
in response to your
roaring voice. Then suddenly
out of fear
or just plain stupidity
I too
begin to step in your direction.
I thrust my chest forward,
transfix an angry stare
and fasten my feet to the ground
on which they stand.

CHOLO

Hey, ¡carnal!
Got'n extra smoke?

CARNAL

We look each other straight in the eye
Exchange glances
And I begin to think

"your carnal to give you
a goddamn smoke
but your prey to kill in all circumstances
otherwise."

Our native ancestors would never trade tobacco

under these circumstances!

I wanna beat you,
demoralize and
dehumanize you.

Tell you, "Sabes qué,
carnal, I think

que estás bien atrocious."
Go off and give you a taste of
my
outlawed, freak of nature, Zapatista rebel,
Guadalupana, araña venenosa,
serpiente emplumada, chola drag queen faggitude.
Kill you with my
kiss of death.

But I stop myself.
I think again and I resolve that
hate born from fear
hate bred from hate
hate of any type, period,
can never cure your homophobia.
So I smile, simply,
and honestly reply, "Nah,
it's my last one, carnal."
And I just keep on sucking.

JESÚS ALONZO

(CHOLO and his friends exit. CARNAL looks down the street, smoking his cigarette.)

(BLACKOUT)

(END OF SCENE)

Scene 7

Straight on Queers Infomercial: Video Installment #4

(The scene opens to TESTIMONY JOTO #1 sitting on a couch in his brightly-colored living room.)

TESTIMONY JOTO #1

(Speaking into the camera.) I finished watching *Straight on Queers* for the first time and I immediately saw changes in my modes of response to the ignorance about jotos. As I turned off the video, there was a knock at my back door. It was my neighbor. He came over to borrow a tomato; but instead I gave him fruit from the tree of knowledge!

(The video cuts to a dramatization. The word "dramatization" flashes on the screen in bold letters.)

Hey, Pátzcuaro, come on in. How are you doing?

PÁTZCUARO

(Walking into living room.) I just came over to borrow a tomato, man. I went out to the store right now but a pinche fag made me loose my train of thought!

TESTIMONY JOTO #1

Well calm down, hombre. You wanna talk about it? Here, sit down.

PÁTZCUARO

No es nada, man.

(Video cuts to a voiceover of the scene PÁTZCUARO describes.)

It's just that I stopped in at the gas station to fill up the old Plymouth, and there was this maricón at the register. Just by the way he looked at me, bro, I knew he was gay! But that's cool, dude. You know I don't have any problems with the gays. So I gave the dude a fifty dollar bill and told him,

PÁTZCUARO (Continued.)
(Video cuts to a slow-motion close-up of PÁTZCUARO who suddenly speaks suggestively.) I need you to fill-up my Barracuda. I've got a real guzzler.

(Video cuts back to the living room.)

Then I ran out. Well when I went back for my change, the maricón just kept checking me out, (Video cuts to a close-up of the REGISTER ATENDANT staring suggestively into the camera.) you know, como que quería conmigo. I'm pretty sure he wanted something more.

(Video cuts back to the living room.)

"To hell with that," I thought, "just give me my change." Pues when I went up to the counter, he's all trying to flirt.

(Video cuts to the scene of the gas station REGISTER ATTENDANT.)

REGISTER ATTENDANT
(Indifferently.) Let's see, you were on pump six? Nine? Oh that's right, pump eight. Okay, I owe you four dollars. Put your hand out. Don't be scared, honey! One, two, three, four, four dollars, nice and crisp, just for you!

(Video cuts to a close-up of the REGISTER ATTENDANT accidentally touching PÁTZCUARO'S hand then cuts back to PÁTZCUARO in the living room.)

PÁTZCUARO
And then he rubs his hand with mine! "To hell with that," I said to myself, "I'm going back home to wash my hands." I don't wanna get no freakin' AIDS!

(Video cuts to initial testimony scene where TESTIMONY JOTO #1 speaks into the camera.)

TESTIMONY JOTO #1

Well, that just about did it for me. I knew I couldn't be quiet, especially after watching *Straight on Queers!* Somehow, in my heart, I knew I had the know-how to put this baby in his place con nada más que pure joto sabiduría.

(The video cuts to dramatization. The word "dramatization" flashes on the screen in bold letters.)

And you think he has AIDS because?

PÁTZCUARO

Because, man! Had you just seen him, you would've known...

TESTIMONY JOTO #1

Known squat, honey, just like you right now! You assume he has AIDS because you assume he's a joto. Therefore, he must have AIDS! Well Pátzcuaro, just to inform you, AIDS is not a disease exclusive to jotos; it never was and it never will be. Rates of infection among straight Latino men and women have skyrocketed and they continue to rise at alarming rates. We are all at risk, mi'jo, gay or straight. And do you know why? It is because of ignorance such as that which you just uttered. Furthermore, Pátzcuaro, AIDS is not an airborne disease! You cannot get it from touching an individual living with HIV. The exchange of certain bodily fluids is required for this. So unless your change consisted of four dollars and an unscreened blood transfusion, or four dollars and actual penile penetration of either of your anuses that lacked preventative measures, you have little to worry about!

(Video cuts to close-up of PÁTZCUARO.)

PÁTZCUARO

Dude, you're disgusting!

(Video cuts to wide shot of both men.)

TESTIMONY JOTO #1

No, my friend, you are. And furthermore, the Center for Disease Control does not list soap and water as preventative measures against the infection of HIV!

TESTIMONY JOTO #1 (Continued.)
(Walking to his door.) Now get your filthy ass out of my house!

(PÁTZCUARO exits house. TESTIMONY JOTO #1 proudly turns to
the camera.)

Thank you, *Straight on Queers!* You completely changed my life!

(VIDEO OUT)

(END OF SCENE)

Scene 8

PSA

(At rise, NURSE escorts PATIENT 1 and PATIENT 2 into a modest office humbly furnished with refurbished desk and chairs. NURSE is a middle-aged, seasoned medical professional with a confident demeanor that juxtaposes the nervous energy initially exuded by the two young men. NURSE carries a clipboard with medical paperwork and wears bright smocks that are adorned with cartoon characters.)

NURSE

(To PATINET 1 and PATIENT 2.) Vengan, muchachos, take a seat. We have your test results.

PATIENT 1

Oh.

PATIENT 2

Sure. Ok.

NURSE

It's only natural to be nervous. But don't worry. We're gonna take good care of you. Our Prevention Counselor will be with you in just a moment. He'll go over your test results and explain everything and anything else you need to do. Can I get you some water or something, honey?

PATIENT 2

No, thank you.

PATIENT 1

Estamos bien, gracias.

(NURSE exits. PATIENT 1 and PATIENT 2 watch closely and then exchange glances at one another. They sit nervously in total silence. NURSE watches them for a moment and notices PATIENT 2 begin to rock back and forth as he clenches a medallion of St. Jude that he wears around his neck. NURSE begins to deliver the poem.)

NURSE

Entre preguntas
Inciertas
Con tus dudas crudas
Incitas esta causa tan dura

No sabes que hacer
Y resuelves que
No hay otra
Más que rogarle
A San Judas

Y cuando él no responde
Invocas
A San Lázaro
Nuestro santo de las dolencias
Mi muy amado Babalú Ayé

PATIENT 2

(Suddenly standing up.)
Santito querido,
Do you know who?
Can you tell me when?
Dime, Padre Santo
¿Fue que a mí me dieron
O
Será que yo daré?

NURSE

Pero bien sabes que ni el
Santo más santo
Ni tan solo por ser santo
Puede saber tanto

Así es que
Toma mi consejo
Ya no lo pienses tanto
If you're gonna fuck

To your heart's delight
Papi
Sé
Alerto
Get yourself tested
Y al próxima
Cógelo con cuidado

(Enter PREVENTION COUNSELOR. NURSE briefly goes over the paperwork on the clipboard before they both enter the office where PATIENT 1 and PATIENT 2 still wait. The remainder of the poem is delivered as a conversation between the four characters.)

PREVENTION COUNSELOR

Nadie te juzga
Although no one is ever truly
Judgement free
Ser ser humano
Is only human
And sex
Is only part
Of what you're gonna do
And who you're gonna be

NURSE

Pero no lo tomes a medias
Sex
Is a risky business
And being careful
Is at the core
Of what you need to be

PREVENTION COUNSELOR

You wouldn't cross the street
Without looking
Or put your hands in the flames
While you're cooking

NURSE

Ni menos
Nadarías en un estanque
Lleno de tiburones

PATIENT 2

(To PATIENT 1.)
Por eso
Si vamos a echarnos
Un rollo sabroso entre cabrones
Mi muy buen chulo
Buenote
Papi
Seamos
Alertos
Y cojamos
Con cuidado

NURSE

Pero no basta coger
Con condón
Porque este sólo
Te protege el pollón

PREVENTION COUNSELOR

Es necesario
Combatir la ignorancia
Grave enfermedad
Que penetra a cualquier hoyo
Sin perdón

NURSE

Pues para qué quieres tanta cabeza
Si el saber es poder
Lo que nos da fuerza

PREVENTION COUNSELOR

No hagas del sexo
Un juego de azar
Una rusa ruleta

Get tested
Edúcate
Y
Educa
Has el compartimiento
De tu sabiduría
Tu legado
Tu más suprema furia

NURSE

Papi
Sé
Alerto
Y cógelo con cuidado

PATIENT 1

   (To PATIENT 2.)
Mi punto no es alarmarte
Tan sólo quiero cuidarte
Para poder después amarte
Y con mi alma
Corazón
Y cuerpo
Disfrutarte
Mi chulo
Moreno
Cabrón
Se me hace agua la boca
Tan sólo pensar en ti
Cómo quisiera probarte

JESÚS ALONZO

PATIENT 2

(To PATIENT 1.)
Pero seamos conscientes
Porque sé que las ganas que yo siento
Tú también sientes
Y aunque estamos
Aquí y ahora
En el presente
Tú y yo no tenemos historia

PATIENT 1

Pero
Ambos tenemos pasado

NURSE

El SIDA
Sí da

PATIENT 2

Y debemos cuidarnos

PATIENT 1 AND PATIENT 2

Papi
Seamos
Alertos
Y cojamos con cuidado

PREVENTION COUNSELOR

Y aunque en esta vida
Nada es prometido

PATIENT 1

Tal vez después de hoy
Tú y yo
No tengamos mañana

NURSE

Pero disfrutemos de esta noche

Moreno
Cojámonos
Sabrosamente

ALL

Un futuro
Mas allá de estas ganas

(BLACKOUT)

(END OF SCENE)

JESÚS ALONZO

Scene 9

El baile del condón

(At rise, LOLA, a drag queen dressed in a traditional costume from the Mexican state of Veracruz pushes a heavy crate across the stage. The dress is adorned with purple accents. LOLA stops and places the crate onto an elevated platform, stage left. She opens the crate and pulls out a man's hat, also from Veracruz. She places the hat aside and proceeds to pull out other objects from the crate. They include: a clay jarro, several mangos, a large rattle, a cluster of plantains, oranges, and dildos of several sizes. Lastly, she pulls out bunches of purple condoms, still in their wrappers. She begins to remove the condoms from their wrappers and stuffs them with some of the objects she pulled from the crate. She then decides to blow-up a condom like a balloon. As LOLA struggles to blow the condom, EL BAILARÍN, also dressed in a traditional costume from Veracruz, walks onto the stage. He observes her as he crosses over to the crate. Consumed with her task, she does not notice him and proceeds to blow into the condom.)

EL BAILARÍN
(Picks up the hat and puts it on.) ¡Mi sombrero!

(Startled, LOLA releases the condom, which goes off flying. She acknowledges EL BAILARÍN and is instantly attracted to him as suggested by her body language. As she approaches him, the song "El Cascabel" begins to play and EL BAILARÍN begins to dance. His dance is choreographed in the style of a traditional Son Jarocho. As he dances, LOLA attempts to get his attention by improvising several dance moves, to no avail. She then hands him one of the condom wrapped dildos that he incorporates into his dance. Happy to see this, LOLA continues her dance improvisations around EL BAILARÍN. Near the song's end, LOLA dances to the front of the stage and tosses condoms to the audience. At the dance's end, a slide reading "¡Cógelo con cuidado!" is projected onto a screen. The dancers exit.)

(BLACKOUT)

(END OF SCENE)

Scene 10

Straight on Queers Infomercial: Video Installment #5

(The video opens to a shot of a man covering his face in embarrassment.)

VOICEOVER
Kiss the embarrassment goodbye!

(Video cuts to a shot of a man looking angry.)

Kick your anger to the curb!

(Video cuts to a shot of a man looking speechless into the camera.)

And say goodbye to the silence!

(Video cuts to shot of *Straight on Queers* video display.)

Get the knowhow you deserve and learn to respond to the many ignorant joto slanders plaguing our society.

(Video pans out to a wide shot, revealing the HOST standing next to the video display.)

HOST
With *Straight on Queers*, you will be quiet no more!

(Camera cuts to a different angle.)

How many times has this guy approached you?

(Video cuts to MACHO. He is overly masculine and pompous. He sports sunglasses and accentuates his body by wearing all too tight, form-fitting clothes. He projects a sense of authority.)

MACHO

It's a known fact that jotos sleep around more than they change their socks. And one guy at a time is just not enough for jotos! These guys are so damn promiscuous!

(Video cuts back to HOST.)

HOST

Order *Straight on Queers* today and respond like this tomorrow!

(Video cuts to RESPONDING JOTO speaking to MACHO.)

RESPONDING JOTO

Child, whose world are you living in? And furthermore, who's feeding you your facts? You better watch yourself or you just might get a bad case of indigestion.

(Camera angle changes, cuts to close-up of RESPONDING JOTO.)

Fact number one: jotos are human beings just like heterosexuals. Be it as it is, we have similar needs as you, be they sexual-emotional or sexual-physical. In other words, fool, you and I are not that different when it comes to what we like in the bedroom.

(Camera angle changes.)

Fact number two: promiscuity is not exclusive to the jotería, lest I remind you that the term "playa" was not coined by nor was it designated for jotos.

(Camera angle changes.)

And now, facts number three and four: you ain't that cute, so get the hell off T.V. and your body ain't that tight, so get you some clothes that fits!

(Video cuts back to HOST.)

HOST

Imagine possessing the ability to respond with such wit, courage, and know-how! Well now you can!

(Phone number flashes on screen.)

Simply call 1-800-WYZ-Joto and for just $19.95, plus shipping and handling, *Straight on Queers* will be delivered directly to your front door. So many jotos have already jumped on the bandwagon and are out in the world today, telling it like it is. Don't be left out in silence. Pick up that phone, sister, and order your very own copy of *Straight on Queers*, today!

(Video cuts to TESTIMONY JOTO #2, a docile looking man sitting in a library.)

TESTIMONY JOTO #2

(Meekly.) Before *Straight on Queers*, I never knew what to say when my brothers and coworkers made fun of me for being gay.

(Suddenly confident.) But now I am a new, courageous, vicious-tongued, knowledgeable jota concientizada! So wátchate, honey! You best know what you're saying before you speak to me.

(Peaceful and cheery again.) Thank you, *Straight on Queers*! And thank you, Jotas Concientizadas, Inc. You truly changed my life!

(Video cuts to *Straight on Queers* video display.)

VOICEOVER

Change your life too!

(Phone number flashes on screen.)

Call 1-800-WYZ-Joto. That's 1-800-W-Y-Z-J-o-t-o! For just $19.95, plus shipping and handling, order *Straight on Queers* today and be a fast-tongued jota concientizada tomorrow. Call 1-800-WYZ-Joto today! Say goodbye to the silence and embrace the vigor of pure joto sabiduría. Operators are now standing by.

(VIDEO OUT)

(END OF SCENE)

Scene 11

Shh!, The Reprisal

(At rise, PLAYER 5 stands front center stage. He is dressed all in white and is barefooted.)

PLAYER 5

Shh-it no
I will not be silent
I will not run
I will not hide
I will not translate
I will not apologize
I will not pretend to be something I am not
And
I will not hate myself for being who I am

I will love unconditionally
I will embrace fraternity
Sorority
Humanity
I will create and recreate family
Community

I will live in the here and now
And be present with each breath I take
I will inhale all that is good
I will exhale everything toxic
I will emancipate myself from all that is against me

I will not own the insults
The stare-downs
The muted whispers
The cynicism
Nor the doubts

JESÚS ALONZO

I will rise above the insecurity
I will step out of the shadows
Out of the darkness
I will challenge fear
I will be the yea to your nay
Whenever anyone wants to
Hold me down
Break me down
Tear me down

I will fight fair
I will fight clean
Never hit below the belt
Nor hit with physical strength
I will remember peace
And the power of words

I will stand with my feet
Firmly rooted to the ground
I will weather each and every storm
And reconstruct anything good that's been destroyed

I will rejoice with every victory
Despite its size
I will move forward
But never forget what's behind

I will honor those who came before me
Revere those who walk with me
And help uplift those coming to join me

I will stretch my arms wide open
Offer a helping hand
I will fill myself with love and compassion
Be a source of empowerment
I will be an understanding man

I will carry my bags
Through every door I enter
Conceal my identity no more
And you will know when I've arrived
Because I will celebrate my existence
And celebrate those
Who join my celebration

(PLAYER 5 inhales deeply as he raises his arms overhead in a Reverse Swan yoga pose. As they meet, he clasps his hands loudly. He pauses shortly then begins to slowly lower his arms, exhaling with a deep, loud "Shh." PLAYER 5 stands in Mountain Pose, looking directly out to the audience. After a moment, PLAYER 1, PLAYER 2, PLAYER 3, and PLAYER 4 join him on stage delivering their respective lines to the poem, El Metamorfosis. Like PLAYER 5, they are also dressed in white and barefooted.)

Metamorfosis

PLAYER 1

It begins in a verse:

PLAYER 2

a poem that will be sung.

PLAYER 3

A song that will be danced.

PLAYER 4

A dance that will end.

PLAYER 5

And such is life, or this one at lease.

ALL

The metamorphosis begins here.

JESÚS ALONZO

PLAYER 2

Full thrust forward,

PLAYER 4

We stand on ground zero.

PLAYER 3

We are blue, green, red,

PLAYER 5

copper, gold, and silver;

PLAYER 1

We are out and about

ALL

And without shame.

PLAYER 3

Sin vergüenza

PLAYER 2

So we will write

PLAYER 5

And we will sing

PLAYER 4

And we will dance

PLAYER 1

The poems that turn into the verses

PLAYER 3

We love to dance and sing.

ALL

The metamorphosis has begun

The metamorphosis will continue

(BLACKOUT)

(END OF ACT II)

THE END

Dedicatorias

Para Manuel Solis

I picked up the original version of *Jotos del Barrio* (*Jotos*) from my Media Studies professor's office at Carleton College. It was the end of the Spring Term, 1995, and students were preparing to go home for the summer break.

My enthusiasm was sparse namely because I accepted a summer job at the College that year and was not going home until the end of August. Further constricting my excitement was the large B- weighing heavily on the cover page of *Jotos*. It was written and circled in bold red ink.

"Classic," I thought and stashed the play away in my backpack, refusing to give it any further thought.

"How'd you do in class," Solis asked me in passing. He too was getting ready to leave campus for the summer.

Earlier that term I shared with Solis my idea to write a Chicano Queer themed play as a response piece to our Media Studies class, *Queer Pictures*.

The idea for the play came after our professor dedicated one class period to "multicultural queer iconography." The class was composed of the work of the late poet and essayist, Essex Hemphill and the "unique point of view" in lesbian pornography.

I walked away from the class angry, thinking that this class was absolutely inexcusable on many different levels. The professor's narrow interpretation of multiculturalism simply failed to consider the existence of more than two thirds of our class's population and well beyond that of queer communities across the U.S.

Aside from my anger I had little with which to proceed, however. Although I realized I was a jotito very early in my youth (like six months after my conception), I was recently out of the closet and was myself trying to make sense of a Chicano Queer identity.

That first year of college, after coming out publicly, I began to meet other jotitos who, like myself, were trying to come to terms with their identity. Finding comfort and trust in each other, we exchanged our stories and experiences with one another. Some read like scenes from a play or a movie, others like poems, some like straight-up jokes, and still others were just too painful to bear. Some of these stories etched themselves into the fibers of my heart because it was my voice that resided in their experiences.

As finals approached that Spring in 1995 it became clear to me that it was the stories that I carried with me – some of them mine and some of them borrowed – that could best begin to define my Chicano queer identity; it was these stories that could best inform my professor that we also existed in this country and that our experiences are just as powerful and valid and universal as anyone else's.

To Solis though, I simply stated, "yeah, I'm gonna write a play about jotos for the class final."

Aside from my older brother Juan, Solis is perhaps the first other individual who not only supported my writing but whom I felt looked upon me as a fellow artista. Shortsighted by grades and rankings, however, I only contemplated the B- molding away in my backpack, allowing it to validate the value of my work. Hence, I proceeded to explain to Solis how much my work sucked and how my overall grade and, subsequently, my GPA would suffer as a result.

Solis responded with a half-roll of his eyes and his signature carcajada – his hearty laughter that juxtaposes his quiet, gentle demeanor. This is perhaps my favorite character trait about Solis because each time I hear it, it reminds me of how genuine of a person he is.

Still smiling Solis offered his words of encouragement, reassuring me that the situation was not as dismal as I made it out to be and that most likely our professor did not understand the nature of my work. Then he asked if he could read the play. Or maybe I asked him if he wanted to read it? Regardless of either of these, before the end of the night Solis had a clean copy of the play in his hands. By morning, both Solis and *Jotos* boarded a plane heading home to San Antonio.

Two weeks later I received a phone call from Solis.

"Hey man, what's up," Solis asked after I answered the phone.

"Oh, not much," I meekly replied.

"So have you worked on the play anymore" Solis inquired.

I was taken aback by the question. Was he referring to *Jotos*? Of course he was; I had no other play in the works! But I was done with that. I had turned it in, received my grade, and moved on. The play had filled its purpose in this life. What more was there to work on?

"Um, no. Should I," I asked laughing.

What came next changed the rest of my summer.

Solis went on to explain that he read the play and decided to share it with some local teatristas and the folks at the Esperanza Peace and Justice Center. My stomach turned a bit. I really did not want the play shared with anyone else, especially not people in the arts.

Solis stated that they thought it was an important work. He told me they were excited to know the show was a homegrown piece written by a San Anto jotito. He finished by explaining that the Esperanza wanted to present a staged reading of the show at the end of August; that I needed to begin revising *Jotos* and get it to him when I was done.

The next morning I sat with *Jotos* and read it for the first time since turning it in to my professor. With my ego still deflated, I refused to believe there was any importance in my work. But like each experience in it, my gut commanded that I respect the play in its entirety, much in the same way it taught me to respect my elder relatives in México – though I did not know them well, I knew enough to know they were important to my life and history. And that is how I proceeded with my relationship with *Jotos*.

I arrived in San Antonio via the Greyhound in mid-August. Even after working all summer, I was able to gather only enough centavitos for a 48-hour bus ride home. Seeing my family and meeting up with Solis made the trip priceless, however.

Solis and San Anto was a funny thought, I remember.

One the one hand San Anto was the common thread that brought Solis and me together the first time we met in Minnesota. On the other, Solis was the common thread that brought me back to San Anto from Minnesota. Now here we were, Solis, San Anto, and me united by *Jotos*.

My heart sang.

In the span of a little bit more than one week, Solis took me to parties, bar-b-ques, art openings, the Teatro Guadalupe, and the Esperanza. Each time, he introduced me as, "Jesús Alonzo, the author of *Jotos del Barrio*." And somehow, the person I was being introduced to knew who I was. I quickly learned that this was a close-knit group of local teatristas, filmmakers, and artistas. I was in awe! San Antonio was Chicano arte heaven and San Pedro had saved a place for my play and me. I remember feeling so supported by these individuals who were all excited about my work. Even after all these years, I am still in contact with some of these individuals who continue to support my efforts.

It is amiss to not mention two teatristas whom I met during my homecoming and who supported my work from its inception. The late Alicia Fernández served as the Director of the staged reading of *Jotos*. Although I knew her briefly, I am forever grateful for the care and respect with which she treated the play. At a moment in my life when Chicanos rejected me for being gay and gays (in Minnesota) rejected me for being Chicano, Alicia embraced me in my entirety.

Alicia Fernández, *¡presente!*

The other teatrista I must recognize is the late Frank Ramirez Ontiveros, better known as Franco. To say that Franco supported my work is a terrible understatement because he is in fact part of the machine that propelled my work forward. Franco served as one of the players for the first reading of *Jotos*. Then during the 2002 staged production of *Jotos* he served as a stand-in on opening night when one of our actors did not show up in time for curtain call and again on closing night when another actor was locked away with another engagement. And Franco did this despite coming to both shows as a patron and not being a part of the production team or cast! Finally, he served as the Stage Manager for the 2009 staged production of Miss America: A Mexicanito Fairy's Tale.

Franco Ontiveros, *¡presente!*

It is also amiss to say that I did not struggle emotionally after going back to Carleton after this first experience with *Jotos*. After all, I had seen the top of the mountain! And although it was not clear if I would ever return to San Anto, I knew it would always be home to me, and to *Jotos*. Manuel Solis saw much more in my work than I ever did and he kept the work alive. It goes without saying that if not for him, *Jotos* might never have found a voice or a home. Likewise, I too might have never found my voice as a joto playwright.

Solis, you are my baby daddy, and who better to fit the bill!

Para María Alejandra Ibarra

It is another phone call. It is the autumn of 2001 and my flip-phone reads that Solis is on the other end. He tells me about Madmedia Productions, a multimedia and multidisciplinary performance collective in town. I caught their first major production, *Pocho/a* at the then Jump-Start Theater in 2000. It starred one of my best friends from high school, María Ibarra and her two male counterparts, Eli Rios and Nicolas R. Valdez. The last I heard, María and Eli had got together and had a baby. María's cancer had also come back, but she was winning the fight once again, though there were some frightening moments.

"How is María doing, Solis," I asked.

"She's good mi'jo," Solis began to reply. "You know how it goes," he finished.

And I did, somewhat. It was during the winter term of my last year at Carleton in 1998 that my mother called to tell me the news. She ran into María's mother at the grocery store or the mall – I can't remember – and la Señora Ibarra told her about María's diagnosis. And although I felt helpless being so far away from María, I quickly learned that she was way more chingona than I ever gave her credit for being. María not only fought cancer head on, but she also refused to let it keep her from the things she loved, namely the theatre and her friends, or stop her from reaching her goals.

I remember visiting her after coming home from college. Light and love always seemed to surround María. Laughter was central. The mood was always light and joyous despite the very real and difficult fight in which she was engaged.

"So I want to share some news with you," reported Solis.

Unsuspectingly I listened.

Madmedia Productions wanted to produce *Jotos del Barrio*. The show was slated for sometime in the spring of 2002 at the Jump-Start Theater. They already had a director in mind, a straight Chicano teatrista who was "so down to do the show," and possibly María Ibarra could serve as the assistant director. Could I please get the script ready and get a copy to him so that he could get it to

Madmedia. There would be a public reading of the script very soon, "just to hear how it sounds and to get some audience response. Cool?"

And just like that, *Jotos* resurfaced once more and was on its way to production.

Although I do not remember why I initially agreed to do the show, I do remember being instantly scared about the notion of people knowing that I wrote it. I sincerely was honored and wanted the show to get produced. I just did not want to be associated with the production. My fear was so great, in fact that I simply gave Solis a copy of old script and refused to attend the public reading and audience response.

It was after this reading that I began to revise the script for the first time since its initial public reading. I gave it to the director and met with him shortly thereafter. He appeared concerned and uneasy. There was nervous laughter and some almost-insulting presumptions about the discernibility of me being a self-taught writer. There was fixation. Particularly regarding a poem that compares my likes in men to my likes in ice cream flavors and which ends with the orator having a full-blown orgasm.

"Yeah. Uh. Mmm? It just doesn't belong in this show, " he suggested.

I thought about it. I laughed. I agreed. That particular poem really did not belong with these particular stories.

There was still great uncertainty from the director, however. I felt it as I left our initial meeting. A week later the poem is out of the show and so is the director – the first by my choosing, the latter by his choosing. He gave no reason and I never saw him again. I realized his uncertainty had another name: discomfort.

The news came by way of Solis. Our "way down" Chicano teatrista director was out but María, despite being in recovery from her cancer and having a toddler to look after, agreed to take on his post. *Jotos* was the first show she would direct and she was ready to take on the challenge. She was not going to let the show fail.

Fail, the show did not. From the first day of taking on the director's post, María demonstrated a keen understanding of the script's strengths and, more importantly, of the things it lacked. Furthermore, she demonstrated her commitment to the show's success through the care, the understanding, and the compassion with which she approached every piece.

Under María's direction *Jotos* experienced several key transformations. First of all, María took one look at the script and immediately put me to work on it's formatting. As a self-taught playwright, I had no formal training on this part of script writing. She quickly guided me through some of these aspects, always emphasizing its importance for the sake of readability and understanding for the director, the actors, and the stage crew. María also changed the order of several of the pieces in order to create continuity and cohesion throughout the entire play. In doing so, María helped me create a multi-faceted, multi-layered experience by carefully piecing all the stories together.

It was during this transformation period that I also added other pieces to the script. These newly added poems and stories were informed primarily by the experiences I had since the first writing of *Jotos*. These experiences span from the HIV/AIDS outreach work I did in México, Los Angeles, and Brasil, to living a closeted life, to my first experience with love, to the fear I felt of being outed an subsequently loosing my job as an educator of young children. Needless to say, *Jotos* doubled in length and now looked more like a play than the angry term paper it was originally set out to be.

If I credit Solis for being my baby daddy, then María is most definitely the mother who birthed *Jotos* the show. Her loving hand and her vision are present throughout the entirety of the script. Her devotion to the script, to the show, and to the cast and crew of the 2002 production are marked with her love and respect. María is an amazing actor, director, mother, wife, teacher, friend, confidant, and visionary. And she not only taught my niño malo how to walk. She taught *Jotos* how to run.

¡Mil gracias María!

Para Erica Salazar

"Is this your show," asked Earnest, waving the flyer for open auditions in my face. He was a fellow bilingual teacher from another campus at the district in which I taught.

"What," I yelled back.

It was difficult to hear him over the loud dance music playing. We were at the Saint, San Antonio's drag show headquarters. It was late and that night's show was over. The young jotitos and lesbianitas around us took to the smoky dance floor as last-call drinks and the smell of slut-walk sex poured around us.

Solis and I were passing out flyers for the *Jotos* auditions at the various gay bars along Main Ave. We hit all the bars that night, and no one seemed to have any interest in the auditions despite our glossy postcard flyer that pictured a local stripper lying in bed with a molcajete between his legs. Two tomates and a big chile jalapeño nestled in the volcanic stone bowl that covered what appeared to be his naked midsection.

"Is this your show," repeated Earnest.

I smiled nervously.

"I didn't know you were a playwright," he gloated.

I tried to remain humble and indifferent. I looked over to the bar in anticipation of the beers Solis and I ordered.

Then he said, "My friend wants to audition for the play."

"What," I exclaimed, no longer indifferent but in fact quite interested.

"Can I introduce you to her," he finished.

I looked at Solis, handing him his beer.

Earnest turned and lead us to the Saint's back bar adjacent to the dance floor. I remember this walk now more like a long trek. Our flyers in one hand, our beer in the other, off Solis and I went in search of this mystery woman – the only human being at the gay bars that night who cared to audition for *Jotos*. We meandered between people. Walked from one room to the next, our pupils dilating from the smoke and darkness. As we trailed in and out of the shadows, Earnest disappeared and then reappeared, over and over again. More smoke. The music became even louder. The crowd became even larger. The back bar came into sight. Earnest turned to look at us.

"There she is," he said excitedly.

We continued our approach. I looked. The smoke began to clear and my eyes regained their focus.

"He's the playwright," informed Earnest, pointing at me with the auditions flyer.

A gentle hand reached out to greet me. Stepping out of the smoke and darkness, Earnest's friend kindly stated, "Hi. I'm Erica."

Fireworks shot from my heart. This was unreal.

"I told him you want to audition for his play," reported Earnest.

"I do," smiled Erica.

My knees buckled. I turned to Solis. Did he see what I saw? It was Erica Andrews standing before us, her long beautiful jet-black hair perfectly slicked back. She wore a black cocktail dress and black stilettos. She held a clutch under one arm and a martini glass in the opposite hand. She was gorgeous!

My heart raced. Frenziedly, I glanced at Solis. Did he hear what I heard? It was Erica Andrews telling me she wanted to audition for *Jotos*.

Fireworks shot from my heart. This *was* real.

But I remained cool, though. I pretended to be unfazed by the whole "Erica Andrews" thing. I gave her directions to the Jump-Start and a little more information about the play. She shared that she never acted before but that she wanted to give it a try. She told us she was nervous and I laughed because I was doubly nervous: I also had never done a play before and now Erica Andrews was auditioning for it! Shortly thereafter Solis and I bid farewell and left the Saint. It was not until we were out of plain sight that I let out my much-suppressed excitement.

"Are you kidding me, Solis," I jubilantly asked. "She don't need to audition. Homegirl can have any damn role she wants!"

Solis replied with his trademark carcajada.

The night of auditions came and we gathered at the Jump-Start knowing that only one person might come, Erica. Gladly though, that was not the case. As the end of auditions neared, however, Erica was nowhere in sight. I stepped out of the theater house to have a cigarette and noticed a woman in the parking lot. She seemed unsure of being at the right place and looked around in all directions trying to figure out which of the several buildings at the Blue Star Arts Complex she needed to go to. Suddenly she noticed me and walked over my way.

"I'm sorry I'm so late," she said with an air of familiarity, as if I was expecting her.

I looked her over quickly, trying to place her. She wore faded-wash jeans, a plain t-shirt and white Keds. Her auburn hair was shoulder length and pulled back in a simple ponytail. She wore no make-up. She appeared frazzled, nervous even. I did not know who this lady was.

"Are the auditions still going on," she continued.

I directed her inside the theatre and stayed out to finish my smoke. I was waiting for our superstar. I really was not interested in this lady's audition. As I took the last drag from my cigarette, though, I came to terms with the notion that Erica was perhaps a no-show. "Maybe it was all too good to be true," I thought to myself as I reentered the theatre to catch the last of our auditions.

"Are you ready," María turned back, asking the frazzled woman from the parking lot. She was sitting in the audience reading over the script.

"Sure," she said and made her way to the stage, script in hand. I admit it seemed that the stage was all too large for her to fill.

"Hi," she said, pausing to smile at us. "My name is Erica Salazar," she continued.

I took a closer look. Suddenly I realized that it was Erica Andrews. She came as herself. And despite the fact that we expected her alter ego to audition, it was Erica Salazar who knocked the audition out of the park.

Listening to her speak Spanish was breathtaking! She spoke it with such ease. She spoke it with such pride. Her entire body moved, almost radiated as she spoke what I later came to learn was her native language. She instantly found herself in the characters, transgender, female, and male. She immediately became the thread that would stitch the pieces of the play together. I think everyone present would agree that the stage had become too small for Erica by the end of her audition.

But Erica just did not awe us at her audition, though. No. Erica continuously amazed us throughout the entire production process. She was first and foremost a professional in the manner that she treated her role(s) and responsibilities as a cast member. Being a leader was natural to her and she quickly set the example for other cast members. She took each note, each critique, and built from them. She met deadlines. She kept commitments. She reached out and helped whomever and wherever help was needed. She connected people and resources to each other, bringing in our second gay cast member, monetary donations, media exposure (which she graciously handled for me like a pro), and even wardrobe and make-up from her own closet. And despite her accomplishments — her then recent titles and crowns — Erica was at all times humble.

As I look back, I remember everything Erica did for *Jotos* and then everything she did as the lead in Miss America. Just before she passed, I wrote a monologue based on several life experiences she shared with me over the course of several conversations. I wanted to honor her courage as a transgender woman and as a proud Mexicana. I find comfort knowing she was able to read the first draft and liked it. More importantly, it gives me great pleasure to be able to honor my friend and to preserve her memory through theatre, where many of us were lucky to meet the real Erica Salazar — the joker, the loving sister, the caring daughter, the courageous mujer, the giving friend, the hopeful Romantic, the story-teller, the versatile actor who forever lives in the voices of *Jotos del Barrio.*

Erica Salazar, *¡presente!*

About Jesús Alonzo

Jesus Alonzo is a self-taught Chicano joto playwright, poet, and storyteller originally from the Southside of San Anto, Tejas. In his writing, Alonzo explores issues of identiy as they relate to race, culture, class, education, language, immigration, gender, and sexual orientation. Drawing inspiration from his father and the Mexicano sensibility for albures (sexually charged puns, or double entendre), Alonzo enjoys using humor as a literary element for inviting audiences to examine the real life struggles his characters must face.

Alonzo is also the author of *Jotos del Barrio* and *Miss America: A Mexianito Fairy's Tale*, also produced and presented at the Esperanza Peace and Justice Center in 2009.

Alonzo earned a Bachelor of Arts in Latin American Studies from Carleton College in 1998 and a Masters of Arts in Counseling from the University of Texas in San Antonio in 2006. Alonzo is an avid runner/half-marathoner working hard to become a marathoner, long-time public school educator, bilingual education teacher and advocate, and a school mental health professional. He currently resides in San Antonio, TX, with his mero-mero-life-compañero, their family of two cats, Autumn and Pimienta, and his personal life coach/dog, Nico Spitzer.

OTHER KÓRIMA PRESS TITLES

Amorcito Maricón
        by Lorenzo Herrera y Lozano

The Beast of Times
        by Adelina Anthony

Brazos, Carry Me
        by Pablo Miguel Martínez

The Cha Cha Files: A Chapina Poética
        by Maya Chinchilla

Ditch Water: Poems
        by Joseph Delgado

Empanada: A Lesbiana Story en Probaditas
        by Anel I. Flores

Las Hociconas: Three Locas with Big Mouths and Even Bigger Brains
        by Adelina Anthony

Joto: An Anthology of Queer Xicano & Chicano Poetry
        edited by Lorenzo Herrera y Lozano

The Possibilities of Mud
        by Joe Jiménez

Tragic Bitches: An Experiment in Queer Xicana & Xicano Performance Poetry
        by Adelina Anthony, Dino Foxx, and Lorenzo Herrera y Lozano

When the Glitter Fades
        by Dino Foxx

36557726R00090